More Praise for *Overfished Ocean Strategy*

"Amid the sea of dry sustainability books, *Overfished Ocean Strategy* is a forceful tide of cutting-edge business stories and essential facts brought vividly to life. Zhexembayeva writes with passion and experience about radical business strategies for a smarter, not just greener, world. She engages our senses and emotions to deliver the broad brushstrokes of what it will take to succeed in the future in business. A brilliant and refreshingly fast-paced read!"
—**Chris Laszlo, Associate Professor of Organizational Behavior, Case Western Reserve University, and coauthor of *Embedded Sustainability***

"*Overfished Ocean Strategy* delivers five simple principles for transforming business, not just through the next generation of sustainability but through truly smart innovation. All those who want to create new market space while creating deeper meaning for themselves and customers need to read this book."
—**Soren Kaplan, author of *Leapfrogging* and speaker, consultant, and entrepreneur**

"To bring three billion new middle-class consumers into the global economy will require a revolution in resource productivity in everything from farms to fisheries to factories. Zhexembayeva's groundbreaking book provides a road map for turning resource scarcity—the 'overfished ocean'—into a competitive advantage. She shows how forward-looking businesses are already doing this and explains how any business can do the same."
—**Joel Makower, Executive Editor, GreenBiz Group, Inc., and author of *Strategies for the Green Economy***

"This is the best sustainability business book of the decade, no question, because it is truly a business book—it's not about sustainability as an add-on but the future of a sensational business model innovation. If you want to lead in the circular economy, inspire new sources of value, and consistently create uncontested market space, place this book at the core of your breakthrough performance agenda. 'This is what I've been looking for for a long time'—that's exactly what I think you are going to say when you read this stunning and special book."
—**David L. Cooperrider, Fairmount Minerals Professor and Faculty Chair, Fowler Center for Sustainable Value, Weatherhead School of Management, Case Western Reserve University**

"If you are looking for a recipe against sustainability fatigue, this book is definitely an eye-opener. Dr. Nadya Zhexembayeva makes a clear analysis of the need for a real radical, disruptive innovative approach to cope with resource scarcity. She does not aim to offer quick fixes, but she does recommend a strong thinking framework. Her business examples are intriguing and hopeful. She definitely offers the sustainability debate a new meaning and businesses the appetite to consider new business models. Refreshing!"
—**Wilfried Grommen, Chief Technologist, Hewlett-Packard**

"A resource-depleting world such as the one we currently live in entails a radical shift toward new governing principles, innovative ideas, and creative mindsets. It means taking a step back from the traditional linear economy, where everything is consumed and subsequently wasted, and finding the 'disruptive innovation' (as the author skillfully names it) that transforms the line into a circle. This book provides the set of rules that will guide you in taking this leap of faith, while telling the inspiring stories of the ones who have already done so. As CEO of an oil and gas company that has placed 'resourcefulness' as the stepping-stone of its strategy, I strongly recommend this book as an absolute must-read for any business professional ready to embark on this challenging but rewarding journey."
—**Mariana Gheorghe, CEO, OMV Petrom, and one of *Fortune* magazine's "Most Powerful Women: The International Power 50"**

"This book gives us five clear principles for business strategies that make sense, bring hope, and stand a good chance of success. This is a book in the new paradigm: beyond the weighty responsibilities of sustainability, here we have practical guidance and clear examples of opportunity enough for every entrepreneur and corporate reformer. This is the strategy text for now!"
—**Jonathan Gosling, Professor of Leadership Studies, University of Exeter Business School, and coauthor of *Nelson's Way***

"What would happen if a smart researcher and businesswoman wrote a book on the broken state of our global economy and how to set it right? In the best case, the outcome would resemble the artful storytelling and crisp advice Nadya Zhexembayeva delivers us in *Overfished Ocean Strategy*. We need every person inside business and out to read Nadya's book today. The good news: in doing so, readers will not only learn key principles for enabling a flourishing future but enjoy the process along the way. Kudos to Nadya for this fresh addition to the short list of truly hopeful and helpful guidebooks to the 21st century!"
—**KoAnn Vikoren Skrzyniarz, founder and CEO, Sustainable Brands**

"When the question is not *if* but *when*, our responses in past decades have been more like the ocean's waves rather than tsunamis. Today, at the edge of the tipping point, businesses, shareholders, and governments need nothing less than the 'Hitchhiker's Guide to the New Reality.' Some of the guidance we need is revealed here in this book. Nadya Zhexembayeva provides exquisite navigation through fundamental questions of meaning and of real needs, through the search beyond the boundaries of risk and of opportunities, and toward radical change. Enjoy the journey and hope to see you in the New Reality."
—**Andreja Kodrin, founder and President, Challenge:Future**

OVERFISHED OCEAN STRATEGY

To Joe
with warm
wishes !

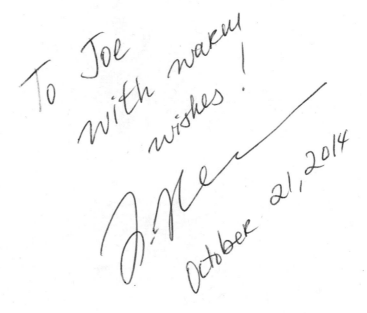

October 21, 2014

NADYA **ZHEXEMBAYEVA**

OVERFISHED OCEAN STRATEGY

POWERING UP INNOVATION FOR A RESOURCE-DEPRIVED WORLD

BK

Berrett–Koehler Publishers, Inc.
San Francisco
a BK Business book

Berrett-Koehler Publishers, Inc.
235 Montgomery Street, Suite 650
San Francisco, CA 94104-2916
Tel: (415) 288-0260   Fax: (415) 362-2512   www.bkconnection.com

ORDERING INFORMATION
Quantity sales. Special discounts are available on quantity purchases by corporations, associations, and others. For details, contact the "Special Sales Department" at the Berrett-Koehler address above.
Individual sales. Berrett-Koehler publications are available through most bookstores. They can also be ordered directly from Berrett-Koehler: Tel: (800) 929-2929; Fax: (802) 864-7626; www.bkconnection.com
Orders for college textbook/course adoption use. Please contact Berrett-Koehler: Tel: (800) 929-2929; Fax: (802) 864-7626.
Orders by U.S. trade bookstores and wholesalers. Please contact Ingram Publisher Services, Tel: (800) 509-4887; Fax: (800) 838-1149; E-mail: customer.service @ingrampublisherservices.com; or visit www.ingrampublisherservices.com/Ordering for details about electronic ordering.

Berrett-Koehler and the BK logo are registered trademarks of Berrett-Koehler Publishers, Inc.

Printed in Canada

Berrett-Koehler books are printed on long-lasting acid-free paper. When it is available, we choose paper that has been manufactured by environmentally responsible processes. These may include using trees grown in sustainable forests, incorporating recycled paper, minimizing chlorine in bleaching, or recycling the energy produced at the paper mill.

Library of Congress Cataloging-in-Publication Data
Zhexembayeva, Nadya.
Overfished ocean strategy : powering up innovation for a resource-deprived world / Nadya Zhexembayeva.
    pages cm
 ISBN 978-1-60994-964-8 (hardback)
 1. Sustainable development. 2. Recycling (Waste, etc.) 3. Scarcity. 4. Green marketing.
 5. Natural resources—Management. I. Title.
   HC79.E5Z4483 2014
   658.4'083—dc23

                                                         2014009525

First Edition
19 18 17 16 15 14   10 9 8 7 6 5 4 3 2 1

Cover Design: Wes Youssi, M80 Design
Interior design, illustration, and composition: Seventeenth Street Studios
Proofreader: Laurie Dunne
Indexer: Richard Evans

To the two most amazing Jernovois of my life:

Lila and Vladimir

Contents

Warm Greetings!

Wherever these words find you today, I hope that there is a good cup of coffee or a heartwarming glass of wine at your side.

This is a selfish hope. We are here to explore a topic that is far from straightforward. And if you have not figured this out yet from any other readings on strategy, change, and sustainability, I am sure that by the end of this book I will have gotten you thoroughly confused. This is an essential part of my job.

I don't mean it lightly. If I ask myself what my job is as an investor, as a manager, and definitely as an academic, my number one job is asking the right questions. And the job of asking the right questions means getting yourself constantly confused. Like many other people, I get so attached to one answer, grow so sure about the rightness of my own choice, that the need to ask any more profound questions disappears. But the change that the world faces right now requires deep questions. Believe me, we will all need that glass of wine!

THE ONLY WAY SOME of us exercise our minds is by jumping to conclusions.

CULLEN HIGHTOWER
WRITER

We live at a time of remarkable transformation. The linear throwaway economy of today—where we extract resources, process them, use them barely once, and trash them immediately as we would a cheap plastic fork—is coming to an end. We are, simply put, running out of things to mine and places to trash. And the market is beginning to recognize it as well: after an entire century of falling costs of raw materials, the first 10 years of the new millennium have seen a whopping 147 percent increase in real commodity prices.[1] Do you happen to be one of millions of managers fighting the ever-rising prices of raw materials, transportation, operations, and more? Welcome to the future!

Kyle Wiens, CEO of iFixit, the largest online repair community, and founder of the software company Dozuki, describes this transformation with laserlike precision: "The economy is broken. It's not because of partisan bickering or the debt ceiling. It's not because there is too much government spending or too little, too many taxes or too few. The problem cuts much deeper than that; it's systemic and it's global. The economy is broken because the principles that make the marketplace thrive will eventually destroy it."[2]

A new economy is being born, one that takes the line and turns it into a circle. At the end of the life of a product, all of the waste comes back into a production cycle as a valuable resource, infinitely. With that comes a new economic order, where we compete and win using a radically new set of rules. For decades, companies claimed their victory by finding the best spot—a unique position on the crowded competitive landscape.[3] Others strived to avoid the crowd by discovering a new market space—swimming into the "blue ocean" waters far away from shark-filled blood-red existing markets.[4]

But this old economic order is running its course. Whether red, blue, or rainbow, the oceans are getting empty, and those managers who deeply understand and master this shift are able to turn the new reality into disruptive innovation and remarkable competitive advantage. As they ride ahead of the wave, new products, new business models, new markets, and new profits follow. Overfished Ocean Strategy is for everyone who wants to survive and thrive in this new

economy: people who are looking for new solutions to their managerial challenges, entrepreneurs and business leaders eager to protect
their companies and get ahead of the wave, journalists and academics
searching for a new level of discussion, educators interested in connecting the dots across disciplines and generations, nonprofit leaders
trying to understand and engage with the new business world, and
perhaps most important, young people around the world who will
become the generation responsible for making the new world work.

All this talk about resource depletion might be making you yawn,
cringe, and recall the recent "green business" craze. No doubt many of
us suffer from "sustainability fatigue." So let me make one thing perfectly clear: Pursuing the Overfished Ocean Strategy is a far cry from
the sustainability efforts that result in "green" products that are (let's
be frank!) ugly, poorly perform, and are grossly overpriced. The world
deprived of resources demands a far more radical change than apolo-
getic compromises or PR nods to the environmentalists. The new era
belongs to an entirely new set of approaches and competencies. It is
time to leave bolt-on and Band-Aid forms of sustainability in the past
and look into a future filled with change of remarkable magnitude—
and promise.

In this book you will learn the new rules of the trade—five essential principles that are becoming increasingly more important for individuals and companies alike: (1) from line to circle, (2) from vertical
to horizontal, (3) from growth to growth, (4) from plan to model, and
(5) from department to mind-set. Together, these approaches inspire
fundamental change and power up radical innovation across countries
and industries—and my task is to make them work for you too.

A few remarks about the flow of this book. The five principles
mentioned above lie at the center of the Overfished Ocean Strategy
and thus will serve as the core of this story. As I am, first and foremost,
a business owner and a manager, stories and cases make up the bulk
of the discussion to serve as practical illustrations of how to make the

principles work. At the end of the chapter for each of the five principles is a short list of tools and resources you might consider when building your own Overfished Ocean Strategy tool kit.

Yet to get to the principles themselves, we first must examine the big trends that are driving global economic transformation and setting the stage for the new rules of competition. Thus, we will first look at the oceans of disappearing resources, overflowing landfills, and new business ideas. Then, we will look at the death of "green" and ponder the sustainability of our marriages (that is no joke!). Real stories of real businesses will help us to navigate throughout. That is the plan.

————————

I started working on this book at exactly 3:18 p.m. on a cold February afternoon in the winter of 2012, standing in front of a group of executives, ready for my strategy talk. The sun had started its descent, and the faces of the business leaders in front of me seemed to be in perfect harmony with the expanse of snow outside the window: cold and motionless. My challenge was simple: to make the invisible visible. The good news was that the journey of discovery had much to offer to the strong minds there in front of me: bankers, car manufacturers, pharmaceutical stars, and traders. While most of the world (including the leaders in my room) remains in the dark, Microsoft is researching a way to turn data servers into residential furnaces—saving millions on cooling off data centers while providing a crucial utility to homes across the world. FLOOW2 is making money by allowing businesses to sell their temporary overcapacity—underutilized machines, skills, and real estate—all with the click of a button. Puma is getting rid of shoe boxes in favor of the remarkable intelligence of the light and reusable Clever Little Bag, while BMW has stopped selling cars and is now selling mobility, electricity included. In Peru, the first billboard that converts air into drinkable water has gone up, while in the Netherlands, wasteful party confetti biodegrades and grows into wildflowers. It was my job to tell these stories—and share the secrets of innovation that make each of them work. So off I went: "We live amid remarkable—though largely undetected—transformation . . ."

Whether these pages find you on a sunny summer day or a cold winter afternoon, my task is still the same. This book is here to make the new competitive reality visible—and to share the best examples of radical innovation for the resource-deprived world. I am deeply thankful to all the executives and businesses that have been my partners for over a decade, and to those who continue to open their doors to my questions and quests. The ocean of resources and ideas is getting overused, but as many of these pioneering businesses show, there is plenty for all of us. To discover the abundance of the future, we first need to recognize the scarcity of the present. To start our journey, we travel to the shores of New England in pursuit of one key question.

Where are the fish?

CHAPTER 1

Where Are the Fish?
The New Competitive Reality

AT A GLANCE

FOR MOST OF THE history of modern business, we have
enjoyed falling prices on nearly all raw materials,
which has made us dangerously oblivious to the shaky
foundations of our global market economy. But the
tides are turning: the new era is upon us. It is time
to look into the facts—and to prepare a strategy for
dealing with them.

Like his father and grandfather before him, Al Cattone has been living off the sea for all his life. For the Gloucester fisherman who spent over 30 years braving the Atlantic's waters, fishing is "not so much a job as it is an identity."[1] But this legacy is coming to abrupt end. In light of extreme declines of cod stocks, the New England Fishery Management Council voted to slash cod catch rates by 77 percent in the area from Cape Cod to Nova Scotia. The destruction of fishing communities across the region is expected to follow, with a domino effect on seafood processors, wholesalers, distributors, and retailers—an entire industrial ecosystem. But the unpopular move is backed by the harsh reality that the cod stocks today are very far from healthy, with some communities netting a bare 7 percent of moderate targets set by the National Oceanic and Atmospheric Administration.

In his struggle and sadness, Al is not alone. In the United Kingdom, the modern fishing fleet must work 17 times harder for the same catch as its sail-powered 1880s counterparts.[2] In northern Japan, the entire fishing industry has been in "terminal decline," with the 2011 tsunami only accelerating the collapse.[3] Recently, the *Financial Times* has become one of the most prominent voices about the fish crisis, warning the world of the decline in fish stocks, which is more severe than predicted. "More than half of fisheries worldwide face shrinking stocks, with most of these in worse condition than previously thought, leading to yearly economic losses of $50bln."[4] And if the proven losses of the present are not enough, the projected losses of the future exceed anything that could be imagined. According to a Stanford University study, overfishing could take all wild seafood off our tables by 2048. "Unless we fundamentally change the way we manage all the oceans' species together, as a working ecosystem, then this century is the last century of wild seafood," warns marine biologist Stephen Palumbi.[5]

In its easy math and empty-plates impact, the story of fish serves as a perfect metaphor for the entire world of resources our economy is built on. Whether it is fish or oil, clean water or gold, vitamin C or helium, the ocean of resources is running dry, and this is creating havoc in the market worldwide. Not one, not two, but three oceans are getting overextended: the ocean of resources, the ocean of waste, and the ocean of ideas. Here is how.

The Ocean of Resources

The question of declining resources is not new. Long before current frameworks, such as the Natural Step,[6] put declining resources at the center of attention, the issue of resource scarcity commanded the notice of theorists and practitioners alike. From Plato[7] in the fourth century BC to Thomas Malthus[8] in 1798 to the Club of Rome in 1972, a parade of esteemed thinkers drew our attention to the looming collapse—to no avail. Hardly any changes in the behavior of businesses, governments, and consumers alike were inspired by their powerful outcry—if anything, the global market grew tired and deaf to the calls for radically new business models. Why?

While the theory of resource decline seemed strong and sound, for nearly two centuries the market reality had been telling the opposite story. McKinsey's 2011 report *Resource Revolution* puts it best:

> Throughout the 20th century, resource prices declined in real terms or, in the case of energy, were flat overall despite periodic supply shocks and volatility. The real price of MGI's index of the most important commodities fell by almost half. This decline is startling and impressive when we consider that, during this 100-year period, the global population quadrupled and global GDP increased by roughly 20 times. The result was strong increases in demand for resources of 600 to 2,000 percent, depending on the resource.[9]

In essence, what the declining prices of resources told us for so long was that we could have our cake and eat it too—grow our population, increase our consumption, and keep cutting prices, all at the same time.

But that was then.

The now looks drastically different—and the speed of waking up to this new reality will determine who will survive and who will vanish in the new era. Each year, I work with about 5,000 senior managers directly, and our conversations so far suggest that the majority have not yet fully awakened to this new world of a rapidly collapsing resource base. So here are a few alarm sirens for you—the general trends that are beyond striking:[10]

- Since the turn of the 21st century, real commodity prices increased 147 percent.

- At a minimum, an additional $1 trillion annual investment in the resource system is necessary to meet future resource demands.

- Three billion more middle-class consumers are expected to be in the global economy by 2030, all putting new pressures on resource demand.

The particularities are no less alarming. Whatever key aspect of business—or life—we consider, declining resources are unraveling the very foundation on which we built our economy.

———————

For decades, the energy debate has been struggling with the question of how much oil and other fossil fuel is left, with no agreement in sight. What we do have agreement on are the demand and the cost of energy. By 2030, world energy use is expected to exceed the 2011 baseline by 36 percent,[11] and the past decade has seen a 100 percent increase in the average cost to bring a new oil well on line. The demand and the supply pressures together create a perfect storm for any business—not because we are running out of oil or any other resource but because the price of energy is becoming severely unpredictable.

THE STONE AGE didn't end because we ran out of stones.

SHEIK AHMED ZAKI YAMANI
FORMER OIL MINISTER, SAUDI ARABIA

Figure 1 is a simple visualization of this volatility: using nominal data from the Energy Information Administration on spot prices of a Brent barrel of petroleum, converted to US dollars in August 2013 using the US Consumer Price Index for All Urban Consumers (CPI-U) to show a more realistic picture, I have plotted the price of oil from January 1986 to August 2013. It turned out to be a rather exciting roller-coaster ride!

Imagine that we run a company producing chairs—perhaps the very chair you are now sitting on. Much of the raw materials in the chair are petroleum derived or petroleum dependent. Now, imagine

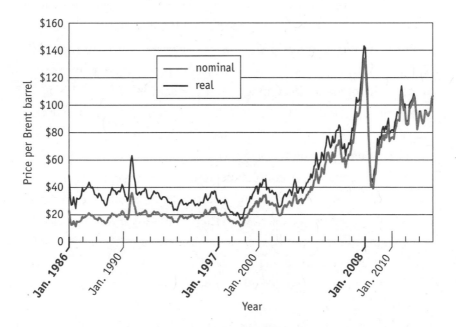

Figure 1. Volatility in Brent crude oil prices from January 1986 to August 2013.

that we are trying to set a sound pricing policy for our beautiful chair—and naturally, we need a somewhat stable cost structure. How do you manage the up-and-down movement in the price of oil—and all dependent products—like what we have seen in the last five years?[12]

If oil prices seem remote to you, the next group of resources cannot possibly leave you uninterested. Do you know anybody who doesn't eat?

ASK NOT WHAT YOU can do for your country. Ask what's for lunch.

ORSON WELLES
ACTOR AND DIRECTOR

Whenever one talks about food, it is assumed that availability is an issue. Yet when 40 percent of food in the United States is never eaten—amounting to $165 billion a year in waste[13]—clearly, when it comes to the developed world, availability is not an issue. Instead, accessibility of food is becoming a strategic concern. Like a nice risotto or rice pudding? Of the top 10 rice-producing countries of the world, the first two—China and India—produce and control more than the other eight combined.[14] If your company or your supplier depends on rice production, such dependency creates real strategic concern, as exemplified by the story of the 2008 global rice crisis. The crisis took place in early 2008, when the international trading price of rice jumped dramatically, increasing more than 300 percent, from $300 to $1,200 per ton, in just four months.[15]

Perhaps rice is not your food of choice, and access to India's resources is far from your business challenges. Yet the global decline of food resources touches every person and every company, if we look at the level of the nutritional content of our most precious vegetable crops. A 2004 study shows an average decline of 20 percent of vitamin C, 6 percent of protein, 16 percent of calcium, 9 percent of phosphorus, 15 percent of iron, and 38 percent of riboflavin from 1950 to 1999 in 43 vegetable crops.[16] We can already foresee a beautiful ripe tomato with absolutely no nutritional value.

A discussion of food leads straight to another essential resource, used in every sphere of business across the global value chain: water.

———

Water is the new oil, says the conventional wisdom of the 21st century. So how much water did you use today?

If you skipped the shower, you might have guessed three to five gallons (or about 10 to 20 liters). A nice bath, and you are probably hitting around 40 gallons (around 150 liters). So what would be the total water count for the day? Fifty gallons, anybody? Or perhaps 100? Think again!

If you had a cup of coffee, some toast, and an egg this morning, you have already consumed about 120 gallons (about 450 liters) of water—enough for three typical baths! And if these words catch you after a nice steak, you might be surprised that a half-pounder would "cost" you a whopping 1,017 gallons (or 3,850 liters)! These calculations are based on the Global Water Footprint Standard,[17] developed through the joint efforts of scientists to allow companies and consumers to deal with the growing water shortages. When it comes to disruption of corporate competitiveness and profitability, the shortages are no joke.

Already today, as the clean water supply is unable to keep up with demand, an estimated 1.1 billion people lack access to safe drinking water.[18] No wonder that Paul Bulcke, CEO of one of the largest food corporations in the world, Nestlé, is calling water scarcity the greatest threat to food security in the future. "By 2030, the demand for water is forecast to be 50 percent higher than today; withdrawals could exceed natural renewal by over 60 percent, resulting in water scarcity for a third of the world's population. . . . It is anticipated that there will be up to 30 percent shortfalls in global cereal production by 2030 due to water scarcity," says Bulcke. "This is a loss equivalent to the entire grain crops of India and the United States combined. . . . Resource shortages lead to price increases and volatility."[19] What a world for us to navigate!

And global water scarcity is only the tip of another gloomy iceberg.

GREEN TECH MAY PROVIDE a way past peak oil. There is no escape from peak water.

GUS LUBIN
JOURNALIST

The year 2012 was tough for the US insurance industry. "From Hurricane Sandy's devastating blow to the Northeast to the protracted drought that hit the Midwest Corn Belt, natural catastrophes across the United States pounded insurers last year, generating $35 billion in privately insured property losses, $11 billion more than the average over the last decade," the *New York Times* reported in May 2013.[20] Much of that bill was covered by the reinsurers—companies that take on insurance policies from primary insurance companies eager to spread out their risk. And if you were an insurance company affected by Sandy, you'd better pray that you had a reinsurer behind you. What about the reinsurers themselves? One of the biggest companies in this business is Swiss Re. J. Eric Smith, CEO of Swiss Re Americas, says of these concerns, "What keeps us up at night is climate change. We see the long-term effect of climate change on society, and it really frightens us."[21]

We might keep debating the science of climate change, going back and forth in politicized discussions of every kind. A stable climate, however, is a key resource for all countries and economies to manage in the years to come. And already today, for one crucial industry—which services much of the global market—the verdict is painfully clear: "For insurers, no doubts on climate change."[22]

Just about now, it would be a good idea for me to stop this doom-and-gloom overview of the upcoming Armageddon. But my hope is that you can see past the challenges to the opportunities. When dealing with a heavy load of data, a wonderful friend and one of the best management professors in the world, J. B. Kassarjan, always offers his clients a magic phrase: "Facts are friendly." Facts are friendly, indeed—and for all the companies pursuing the Overfished Ocean Strategy, they have become a source of competitive advantage. From one set of facts we go to another, traveling from the ocean of resources to the ocean that is getting intensely abused: waste.

WE BUY THINGS WE don't need with money we don't have to impress people we don't like.

DAVE RAMSEY
FINANCE SPECIALIST AND AUTHOR

The Ocean of Waste

As I type these words, the room is filled with light and the smell of peonies. The desk is barely visible under the messy piles of papers and books. An old bag of chips smiles at me from behind the desktop. Always on the move, I have not touched my desktop computer for more than three months. Yet about 1.8 tons of raw materials were used to produce this single machine, which on its own weighs around 30 pounds (14 kg).[23] With this level of utilization, my computer will soon come to the end of its life cycle—we will simply clear up the space, getting rid of the unused device. More than 47.4 million computers were thrown out in 2012 in the United States alone, and no more than 25 percent of those devices were recycled.[24] If we apply that percentage to my 30-pound computer, with only 25 percent of its weight recycled, that means that barely 0.19 percent of all originally mined materials would go recycled.

Fully 99.81 percent would be wasted.

It would be wasted not because the materials mined and processed to build the computers have no value, but rather because we have not been designing products and processes with that value in mind. Our throwaway economy works on the assumption that it is easier to make a new product than to reuse resources already processed. But as we enter the 21st century, "throwaway" is going away. The UK warned that it would run out of landfill space by 2018.[25] Dubai already approached this limit in 2012, when one of its two key landfills reached capacity and was on the brink of overflow.[26] The garbage crises in Naples and Bangalore became so famous that they reached the pages of most major media outlets, the *New York Times* among them.

With global landfills overextended to the very top of their capacity, no wonder that waste overspills in every direction. Most of us have heard of giant waste fields floating in our oceans. While no scientist has provided a definitive calculation of the size of any of the fields (Massachusetts? the Netherlands? the moon?), CNN refers to one such field as an "enormous, amorphous, nasty soup that stretches for hundreds of miles."[27] The title of the article is no less telling: "The Pacific toilet bowl that never flushes." Ready for a swim?

Every time I hear these stories of waste, an impatient pragmatism in me demands: so what? For an environmentalist, the answer to this question might imply activism (and pessimism). But for an entrepreneur and manager, the implication is rather different. Architect and designer William McDonough and the rest of the Cradle to Cradle crowd made it into a simple formula: "Waste equals food." In other words, hundreds of miles of plastic floating in the ocean is an environmental disaster indeed, but it is also a whole bunch of wasted petroleum that could, if approached with intelligence, be turned into a business opportunity. It all depends on the quality of your ideas.

The Ocean of Ideas

A self-made billionaire who starts the Spanx lingerie company from a folding table . . . a 17-year-old who sells his app to Yahoo for $30 million . . . organic baby food started at a UK kitchen sold to an American giant. . . . We have all heard those stories—and (well, I have to speak for myself here) dreamed of being part of them. Could it be that the ocean of business ideas is also running dry?

According to PWC, 2013 started with a 12 percent decline in dollars spent in venture capital investment in the United States and a 15 percent decline in the number of deals.[28] Such a decline is projected or already manifested in a number of US states (such as Ohio) and European countries (France comes to mind first) and runs across many industries. What is the issue?

Sandi Cesko, a Slovenian entrepreneur who grew his company from $70 to $700 million in sales amid global crisis to become an entrepreneurial poster child for a *Harvard Business Review* story,[29] put it this way: "We are going through a major transition. In the past, we sold *products*. Today, we are selling *services*. But the global overcapacity, coupled with resource crunch, means something new. We simply cannot possibly sell more and more stuff. Tomorrow, our capacity to sell will depend on our ability to stay relevant." We will have to sell *meaning*.[30]

Sandi's insights echo the work of business-trend watcher Daniel H. Pink. In his best-selling book *A Whole New Mind*, Dan speaks of the same patterns—or ages—that the global economy has been going through:

> Think of the last 150 years as a three-act drama. In Act I, the Industrial Age, massive factories and efficient assembly lines powered the economy. The lead character in this act was the mass production worker, whose cardinal traits were physical strength and personal fortitude. In Act II, the Information Age, the United States and other nations began to evolve. Mass production faded into the background, while information and knowledge fueled the economies of the developing world. The central figure in this act was the knowledge worker. . . . Now . . . the curtain is rising on Act III. Call this act the Conceptual Age. The main characters now are the creator and the empathizer.[31]

If our ability to compete in the future depends on the ability to create new meaning, how are we to foster *this kind* of innovation?

The Disappearing Line

Swim through the overfished oceans, connect the dots, and you will get to a bigger picture. Think of the global economy in which we are living today as one long line. The line starts with all the companies that are mining, growing, or raising something—those are our only options when it comes to raw materials. The line finishes with all the companies managing a not-very-sexy but increasingly lucrative business: waste. All other businesses—large and small, products and services—are between these two poles. That is our entire global economy. One giant supply chain.

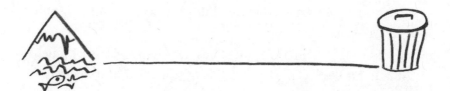

It is *linear*—there is only one straight line from the beginning to the end. It is *throwaway*—as, generally speaking, we use what we mine only once, throwing away most of the resources just the way you throw away a plastic fork after a onetime use. And it is *collapsing*—as we are running out of things to mine and places to trash.

We are in the midst of the transformation of a lifetime.

For most businesses, this transformation is invisible. For those bearing its crushing impacts, it is disastrous. Yet some see it as the greatest opportunity of the 21st century.

TerraCycle is one such business. Known as the company that produced the world's first product made from 100 percent postconsumer garbage, TerraCycle has "outsmarted waste" by engaging more than 20 million people in collecting waste in over 20 countries and diverting billions of units of waste. Now a company that turns waste into over 1,500 different products, TerraCycle was once a laughingstock of the entrepreneurship competition. The first product of the company, founded by a barely 20-year-old Princeton dropout, Tom Szaky, was far from glamorous but made up for it with a great name: Worm Poop. An all-natural fertilizer, Worm Poop is packaged in recycled plastic bottles, which the company collects in part through a US-wide recycling program. The *New York Times'* Rob Walker wrote:

> You don't hear much about worms, or their waste, from the various big-box retailers, globe-trotting pundits and good-looking guests of Oprah Winfrey who appear to be leading the conversation about environmental concern these days. But TerraCycle's plant food is actually a mass-oriented variation on something that hard-core eco-people talk about all the time: the worm bin. Containers filled with shredded newspaper and worms, such bins are used for composting food scraps. Worms eat this waste and digest it, and "compost exits the worm through its tail end," one online guide explains. These "castings" . . . happen to make good plant food.[32]

TerraCycle now sells at major retailers ranging from Walmart to Whole Foods Market. Look who is laughing now!

THE STATUS QUO IS a very powerful opiate, and when you have a system that seems to be working and producing profits by the conventional way of accounting for profits, it's very hard to make yourself change. But we all know that change is an inevitable part of business. Once you have ridden a wave just so far, you have to get another wave. We all know that. For us, becoming restorative has been that new wave, and we have been riding it for 13 years now. It's been incredibly good for business.

RAY ANDERSON
FOUNDER, INTERFACE INC.

There is no question that turning the challenges of the overfished ocean into a vibrant business opportunity is much easier for a start-up than it is for a corporation with a history. Don't get me wrong: I have nothing against the sweethearts of disruptive innovation for a resource-deprived economy, the Body Shops and the Whole Foods Markets of our world, built from the very start on a solid foundation of Overfished Ocean Strategy principles. Yet with all due respect, I often feel that they almost have it easy, and it is the traditional companies striving to transform into a more competitive version of themselves that are up against a real challenge. Of course, it is an immense task to build the world's best vacuum cleaner, but just imagine what it would take to transform that working vacuum cleaner into the world's best TV set? That is the scale and complexity of transformation required here.

Bayerische Motoren Werke AG—also known as BMW—is one such company navigating the murky waters of the resource crunch.

The company moved well beyond selling products to selling services— and from a car company transformed itself into a mobility company. Focusing on mobility—a service rather than a product—allows the company to power up radical innovation and open doors to a completely new business opportunity. Take, for example, the DriveNow car-sharing service, employing BMW i, MINI, and Sixt cars, which allows people in densely populated urban areas to enjoy the benefits of a personal car without owning one. The idea, as BMW explains, is simple: "The mobility concept is based on the motto 'pick up anywhere, drop off anywhere.' Billing is per-minute, fuel costs and parking charges in public car parks are included. Users can locate available cars using the app, website or just on the street. A chip in the driving license acts as an electronic key."[33] Now, that is a service I am ready to explore!

ParkatmyHouse—a strategic investment by BMW i Ventures—is another example of BMW's remarkable resource intelligence and ingenuity. A simple online marketplace, powered by an app, allows people who own private parking places to connect with people who are searching for one. Imagine the savings of time, fuel, CO_2 emissions, and more—and money made—on this simple solution. And for BMW itself, having a stronger parking infrastructure is essential for future sales: if we have good parking, we are ready to drive cars, right?

Mobility services are not the only radical innovation coming out of BMW. In an effort to protect and defend profits, the company decided to harness winds thrashing across eastern Germany to secure power as costs rise as a result of Germany's EUR 550 billion ($740 billion US) shift away from nuclear energy. BMW's transitions seem deceptively simple. Yet when the market forces inspire you to shift your focus from designing cars to designing mobility, disruptive innovation follows; any designer and engineer will tell you that most innovation happens on the verge of the impossible.

Similarly deceptive is the move toward control of the entire energy value chain—but the numbers and the endorsement of business analysts, such as those quoted in *Bloomberg*'s 2013 review, speak volumes.

> At BMW's Leipzig plant, the four 2.5-megawatt [wind] turbines from Nordex SE will eventually generate about 26 gigawatt-hours of electricity a year, or about 23 percent of the plant's total consumption, said Jury Witschnig, head of sustainability strategy at the Munich-based manufacturer. The automaker seeks to eventually get all its power from renewables, compared with 28 percent in 2011—both to cut its carbon output and to benefit from falling prices for wind and solar energy. "There will definitely be more such projects" from renewable sources, Witschnig said. "Energy prices are part of the business case," and in Leipzig, wind power was cheaper than other options.[34]

But that is not all. BMW's rapid marriage with the energy business is a sign of remarkable foresight. As legislation continues to press for fewer and fewer emissions (Euro VI requirements being one such pressure), the movement away from combustion engines appears inevitable. Electric vehicles are one alternative—and judging by the fast pace of model launches in this domain, it seems to be a viable option. Yet when you manufacture combustion engines, the emissions are fully in your control, as your engineers are the ones designing an intelligent (or not so much) motor. When we move to electricity, however, that control disappears, as emissions are now dependent on the efficiencies of power plants. And that is exactly why BMW's tango with energy production is so ingenious: it puts control back in the hands of the company—way ahead of the competition.

Swiss Re is another giant riding ahead of the wave and turning disappearing resources into a thriving business model. The primary product of Swiss Re, a 150-year-old reinsurer with over $33 billion in revenues as of 2012, is insurance for insurers, so the company can hardly be equated with coal-burning plants or methane-producing industries. A company rooted in Swiss rationality and conservatism, the reinsurer surprised the entire industry by taking on the increasing lack of climate stability as a business risk—and opportunity—as early as 1994. By 2007, Swiss Re had introduced a number of financial tools for dealing with the risks associated with climate change. As Nelson D. Schwartz of *Fortune* magazine explained,

> Buyers can bet on future heat waves or cold snaps with puts and calls on specific periods of time and temperatures, much as conventional options have a preset strike price for a stock. So a farmer in India might be able to buy insurance from a local insurer in case the usual monsoon rains fail to arrive, or, conversely, his fields are flooded.[35]

In the following years, the company upgraded its entire portfolio and pricing to respond to the rising costs of climate change. Speaking to Bloomberg TV in 2009, Swiss Re's senior climate advisor, Andreas Spiegel, took no prisoners, estimating weather-related losses at $40 billion annually:

> Weather-related insured losses are rising, and the intensity of weather-related events such as hurricanes is going up as well. We are integrating these risks in our pricing, trying to quantify certain aspects of climate change and integrating them into our models. Climate- and weather-related risks are a part of our core business. More and more, we see this as a business opportunity, as adaptation to climate change is about managing risks in the long term. And that is our business.[36]

————

Whether red, blue, or rainbow colored, whether made of resources, waste, or ideas, our oceans are running dry. We can continue to ignore this trend, falling deeper into the coma of denial along with millions of other businesses. We can run and hide, pushing it to the bottom of the corporate agenda, waiting for a better time to make a move. Or we can turn the overfished ocean into the driving force for radical renewal. So what should business do?

CHAPTER 2

Overfished Ocean Strategy: Five Principles That Make It Work

AT A GLANCE

IN THE ERA OF the collapsing linear economy, the Overfished Ocean Strategy transforms today's depletion of resources into tomorrow's differentiated long-lasting profits. Five principles allow companies to power up innovation for a demanding world.

It is green, dense, and surprisingly light. Fitting perfectly in the palm of my hand, it leaves a light, oily residue on my skin. It is fragrant (just a touch of soft, alluring smell) and textured (it looks like thousands of little worms squished together). It goes against everything we are taught by conventional strategy theory. And it is an amazingly powerful symbol of the new era dawning.

Intrigued? While you are trying to guess what exactly I am holding in my hand, let me set the context to spice up the big reveal.

Popular strategic thought tells us that to compete well, we need to find the most advantageous position in the crowded market space and stick to it. Michael E. Porter is the guru at the helm of this thinking, and his famous menu of "generic" strategies suggests that in the tough search for ideal positioning, we are to make two primary choices.[1] The first choice is between price and differentiation. Do you compete on cost, striving for the most competitive (read cheap) production on the market, or do you have something unique to offer that differentiates you from other, cheaper competitors? The second choice is about focusing your efforts: do you want to target a specific segment (narrow focus) or the entire universe of consumers (broad, global market scope)? The two choices set into a two-by-two grid will present you with four possible options making up the entire landscape of the market to consider.

Play with brands of your favorite product—say, a smartphone—and you will immediately see which strategy is pursued. Today, Apple's iPhone is conquering the market with a unique differentiation strategy—it can hardly be called the most cost-attractive smartphone on the market, but the company is pursuing a broad market scope. The Vertu cell phone, in contrast, is a differentiation-clad product made attractive to a very narrow segment on the market—a luxury brand for a small slice of the consumer pie. The LG Optimus smartphone is a choice that pursues cost leadership—at a price one-tenth that of the iPhone—with a broad, global appeal. Huawei (ever heard of this one?)—the third-largest cell-phone producer on the market[2]—offers the even cheaper Y-300 model targeted at Asia's "ant tribe community," which refers to young people who go to the city for a better life but get stuck with low-paid jobs and high costs to live there.

Once you explore the marketplace and find your own unique position, the question becomes, how do you maintain it? What can you do to preserve your stake? The logical answer would be to keep doing what you are doing—and continue to get better at it. If you are selling a product that is uniquely different, keep pushing it forward and upward; add features; build new bells and whistles, and more of them. If you are going for cost leadership, keep driving down the cost with more efficiencies and better processes. And that is exactly where the problem lies.

IT'S NOT THAT WE need new ideas, but we need to stop having old ideas.

EDWIN LAND
FOUNDER, POLAROID

"For those of you who haven't made a lot of steel, historically there are two ways to make it. Most of the world's steel has been made by massive integrated steel companies. The other way to do it is to build a mini mill. In a mini mill, you melt scrap in electric furnaces, and you could easily fit four of them in this room."[3] The author of an impressive collection of books and one of the most celebrated strategic thinkers of our time, Clayton Christensen is telling a story of disruptive innovation he has shared with thousands before.

"The most important thing about a mini mill is that you can make steel for 20 percent lower cost than you can make it in an integrated mill. Now, imagine you're the CEO of a steel company somewhere. In a really good year, your net profit will be 2 to 4 percent. Here is a technology that would reduce the cost of making steel by 20 percent. Don't you think you'd adopt it?" The answer to Christensen's question is so obvious, it almost turns the inquiry into rhetoric. Yet why is it that no integrated steel companies anywhere in the world have built a mini mill—even though it would save them from bankruptcy, which caught up with all but one integrated mill by 2012? The answer, as Christensen suggests, is the core dilemma for any innovator in any industry, anywhere in the world.

In the steel industry, as in your own industry, many tiers make up the market. The lowest-cost products are at the bottom of the market: for steel, that would be concrete reinforcing bar, or *rebar*. Any company can make rebar, while steel for cars, appliances, and many other pricier products is much harder to produce. Rebar happened to be the only market that mini mills were capable of serving at the beginning. Then, mini mills used scrap to produce steel, and the quality was low. Reinforcement bars get buried in cement, have almost no specifications, and thus can be made of low-quality steel. And thus, mini mills set off to conquer the rebar market with all their might.

What about the integrated mills? Well, they were happy to give up the rebar market. As a commodity, reinforcement bar is a low-margin product, so dropping it would allow for shifting the focus on angle iron and thicker iron and rods and bring home a higher margin.

While the mini mills built-up their rebar capacity, the integrated mills shut down rebar lines—and enjoyed a higher gross-margin profitability. Everyone was happy. The mini mills were enjoying a piece of the pie, while the integrated mills got better performances. And then came 1979.

It was the year when mini mills celebrated their final victory, driving the last of the integrated mills out of the reinforcement bar market. But the happiness was short-lived: the price of rebar fell by a whopping 20 percent. It turned out that a low-cost strategy makes you competitive only when there is a high-priced competitor. With all the high-cost integrated mills out of the game, mini mills had to look for a new way to make money. Making better quality steel was the only way forward—and for the integrated mills, it was a new chance to get rid of another low-margin product. So the story repeated itself again and again.

This climb up the hill to the top of the market—continuous improvement of bells and whistles in products, services, and processes—is what most big companies do as they try to survive. They do exactly as demanded by the customer, trying for a better version of the product, hiking up the market tiers, until there is nowhere else to climb. And at just about that time, a newcomer comes along, offering a completely different—cheaper or more appealing—alternative, sending the big companies down the drain. Remember the story of Kodak, a company that misjudged the charm of digital photography and went bankrupt in 2012? Or how about the struggle of Nokia, once the top-of-the-world producer of cell phones, which failed to notice the growing appeal of smartphones? As with the slow collapse of the integrated steel industry, they, too, were not too big to fall. Christensen calls this all-too-familiar story of old-versus-new "disruptive innovation."

And it is precisely this kind of innovation that I am holding in my hand in Figure 2. So what is it?

Take a close look. A soap bar? A spinach hamburger? A sponge? Some sort of energy tablet? An eco-macaroon? A new-age vitamin pill? A breakthrough detergent? Before you is the equivalent of not one, not two, but *three bottles of shampoo*—all squished into one solid bar. That is the way to disrupt!

What do we sell when we sell shampoo? What end benefit do the customers get? What is the value? Clean hair, indeed. What ingredient need not be supplied to ensure this desired outcome, as it is always available? Water, indeed. So why do we pump water, process water, bottle water, package water, store water, transport water, sell water, and waste plastic post-water to wash our hair, when water is the only ingredient that is not necessary to provide?

That was exactly the starting point for Lush Fresh Handmade Cosmetics, a 20-year-old UK brand, when it started working on

Figure 2. Pop quiz: is this a beauty product, a fertilizer, or something good to eat?

its solid-shampoo line. According to the company, "The inventors worked with Stan Krysztal"—one of the leading cosmetic chemists of Great Britain—"to create these very clever little bars; an effective, hardworking shampoo base, quality ingredients, beautiful fragrances and, best of all, require no packaging. Handy for travelling, compact and easy to use, each bar is roughly the equivalent of three plastic bottles of shampoo. These humble bars are (probably) one of the greatest inventions we've ever come up with."[4] The Lush team loves to talk about it. But what about the customers? Naturally, a number of customers would refuse such a strange-looking shampoo option. My baby brother is one of them. Whenever he visits us in Europe, I have to make a conscious effort to restock his bathroom. "I am a normal person," he claims. "I like my soap solid and my shampoo liquid, and not the other way around!"

Yet by any measure other than my brother's comfort zone, Lush's solid invention has been a great success since its launch in 2007, capturing rave reviews and a solid (pun intended!) customer following. Here is one such review from a rather conventional consumer—a Boston.com writer's take:

> Trust me, I was skeptical too. A rock of shampoo, eh? Sounds about as effective as a steel wool pad as conditioner. But after trying it multiple times at an adult sleepover—don't judge—I slowly became convinced. The stone of shampoo seems to last forever (if you keep it in a dry place after use), and it comes in a variety of scents. I recently picked up cinnamon and clove. But most importantly, it's pretty damn effective. The shampoo itself lathers nicely (sorry to sound like a Prell commercial . . . wait, do they still make that?) and at about $10 a rock, it's a better deal than it appears."[5]

But the glowing reviews and growing revenues are not the only business victories for Lush solid shampoo; on the other side of the business continuum, the company is also doing well with costs. As of 2013, Lush has avoided producing, bottling, and distributing six million plastic bottles globally by selling shampoo bars—count in 2.6 ounces (or 75 grams) of plastic saved per shampoo bar, and multiply that by all the savings in energy and labor costs that would have been incurred designing, producing, bottling, and storing the bottles.[6] Annual water savings from producing the solid shampoos are nearly 120,000 gallons (or 450,000 liters) globally, while transportation savings are beyond surprising: when calculated per wash, transportation costs are *15 times less* than those of liquid shampoo. Additional resource intelligence comes in a form of raw-material savings: the bar has no preservatives, as there is no liquid content requiring preservation. And with a scale of 830 stores in 51 countries carrying the product (which nearly doubled from 2007's 438-strong chain), strengthened revenues and intelligent cost structure for the unusual product are a welcome performance outcome for the once-tiny underdog of the cosmetics industry.

The story of Lush solid shampoo is a story of radical innovation. While the traditional majority of cosmetics companies are fighting for a share of the difficult consumer market with more appealing packaging and stronger advertising campaigns, and while the eco-conscious minority is struggling with recycled plastic and third-party "green" certification, Lush goes well below the surface and delivers an entirely new way of looking at a product. Once a barely known company that started with a sausage machine in the messy workshop of a nearly bankrupt husband-and-wife team, Lush has put into question the essential value delivered by traditional shampoos and paved the way for an entirely new way of thinking.[7] Lush's solid-shampoo bar exemplifies the company's production standards. About 70 percent of the products sold require no packaging, much of the product range has no synthetic raw materials, and over 70 percent of the range is totally unpreserved. For Lush, this approach to resources is simply business as usual. For most of us, it is anything but.

WE ARE CURRENTLY NOT planning on conquering the world.

SERGEY BRIN
COFOUNDER, GOOGLE

In its unexpected take on resource intelligence, Lush is not alone. OMV, an integrated oil and gas company that supplies 200 million people in Central and Eastern Europe with energy, calls it *resourcefulness*. This term, which smells of ingenuity in the age of the Great Recession, captures the new essence of survival. "As one of the leading European oil and gas companies, OMV faces major challenges to which only innovative thinking can be the answer," OMV explains. "Global energy requirements are increasing significantly. At the same time, environmental protection and social justice are of growing importance. The demands placed on us grow as we expand our operations. This is why we made being careful with our resources one of our basic business principles." OMV Resourcefulness Strategy demands that every one of the company's 29,000 employees face the fundamental question of the collapse of the linear throwaway economy—and take it as a productive challenge.[8] As such, it is a strategy that deliberately tackles both *natural* and *human* resources. On one hand, the company runs extensive eco-efficiency and eco-innovation programs to reinvent the way it provides for the energy needs of its customers. Hydrogen (fuel cell) mobility, biofuels, and water and carbon management all are under this umbrella. On the other hand, OMV looks at the diversity, skills, and community engagement of its employees as key resources of the future, and runs comprehensive programs to protect and grow this capital. When I visited the company's biggest refinery in the summer of 2013, I was surprised to learn that even the apprentices—high schoolers striving to get trained and employed by OMV—look at the issues of resources in a broader sense. "We sell something that is disappearing. So the question for us is what to sell next, so that all of us don't disappear, too," said a shy 16-year-old.

Trendwatching.com, the leading consumer trend reporting company, gave the new wave of strategic resource intelligence a catchy name—Eco-Superior. It flagged this trend in 2011 as among its 11 most important consumer demands for the year, and again in 2013 as one that is here to stay. Here is why: "When it comes to 'green consumption,' expect a rise in ECO-SUPERIOR products: products that are not only eco-friendly, but superior to polluting incumbents in every possible way. Think a combination of eco-friendly yet superior functionality, superior design, and/or superior savings." Among the products and innovation highlighted by Trendwatching is the Throw & Grow confetti sold by the Netherlands-based gift store niko niko. The confetti is made of biodegradable material embedded with wildflower seeds; when the confetti is used, it can be left on the ground or discarded onto soil to disintegrate naturally and grow into flowers. Another innovation on the list is a billboard that generates drinkable water—9,000 liters of it in three months—thanks to Peru's University of Technology and Engineering (UTEC). The Torre de Especialidades building of the Mexico City hospital also makes the cut—it now absorbs and breaks down chemicals in the surrounding air. Using Prosolve370e tiles, developed by Berlin-based design firm Elegant Embellishments, the building features tiles painted with titanium dioxide, which interacts with UV light to break down pollution into less toxic chemicals.[9]

Together with Lush, OMV, and Trendwatching.com, Design Hotels elevated the search for innovation for a resource-deprived world to the level of core strategy. A 20-year-old company that represents and markets a carefully selected collection of 250 independent hotels in over 40 countries across the globe, Design Hotels refers to this new strategic effort as Finding Infinity. "We live in the age of sound bites, of short attention spans, of celebrity worship. First-term politicians seem to want only one thing: a second term." Is there a vaccine against our collective short-sightedness? For Design Hotels, there is. With a goal of replacing today's fuels with clean and endlessly renewable alternatives, the company has initiated a "full-speed-ahead-no-time-to-lose movement . . . setting a path for a future based on infinite resources." The company has joined intellectual forces with a number of inventors and change makers, such as a young Australian engineer named Ross Harding, who created Finding Infinity. The resulting program, named "Design Hotels is Finding Infinity," attacks the essential problem of the disappearing linear economy. [10] "The world is powered by fuels that will run out in two lifetimes. This is not our problem—it's our opportunity!" declares the powerful partnership.

Pursuing this opportunity is what I call the Overfished Ocean Strategy.

Overfished Ocean Strategy

In their 2005 blockbuster *Blue Ocean Strategy*, W. Chan Kim and Renée Mauborgne invited the business world to leave behind the crowded waters of the existing market and instead search for—or create demand in—the uncontested market space.[11] "The only way to beat the competition is to stop *trying* to beat the competition. In red oceans, the industry boundaries are defined and accepted, and the competitive rules of the game are known. In blue oceans, competition is irrelevant because the rules of the game are waiting to be set."

Kim and Mauborgne's invitation offered a striking contrast to Michael Porter's positioning concept. With the powerful advice of the latter, companies for decades claimed their victory by finding the best spot—a unique position on the crowded competitive landscape.[12] Following the fresh invitation of the former, other companies strived to avoid the crowd by discovering a new market space—swimming into the "blue ocean" waters far away from shark-filled blood-red existing markets.[13] What a great idea! However, at the core, the "blue ocean" companies studied by Kim and Mauborgne operate and invent within the same resource constraints as their "red ocean" counterparts, oblivious to the collapsing linear economy and all the pressures associated with it. As the linear throwaway economy is approaching its collapse, this *old* economic order is running its course. Whether red, blue, or rainbow, the oceans are getting excruciatingly empty, and those managers who deeply understand and master this shift are able to use the new reality to power up radical innovation and secure a remarkable competitive advantage. As they ride ahead of the wave, new products, new business models, new markets, and new profits follow. Behold the Overfished Ocean Strategy.

A new economy is being born, transforming the collapsing linear throwaway economy into a more lasting, more abundant, more sustainable version of itself. The transformation brings about a new economic reality, where we compete and win using a radically new set of rules. While the companies, people, and projects pioneering these new rules are still rare, there are enough of them to suggest the first few essential principles that allow managers to innovate their way into a new world. Five new rules of the trade—five essential "secrets"— appear increasingly important for individuals and companies eager to power up a new strategic direction and secure the source of a truly sustainable value:

- *One*: From line to circle.

- *Two*: From vertical to horizontal.

- *Three*: From growth to growth.

- *Four*: From plan to model.

- *Five*: From department to mind-set.

Together, these approaches inspire radical change and drive disruptive innovation across countries and industries—and my task is to make them work for you too. In the chapters that follow, I invite you to explore each of the principles in depth and discover companies that have already mastered them. Here is an introduction to this very different—and very hopeful—future.

One: From Line to Circle

The rapid decline of resources—from coal to tuna to vitamin C in a typical tomato—means that one way or another, all of us will have to find a new path forward. That path, however, is not new at all— indeed, it has been perfected over the course of millions of years by nature itself. You see, nature does not have waste. Waste of one process becomes food for another, in perpetual cycle. When an animal dies, its body is not thrown into a landfill; instead, it becomes a source of valuable nutrition for millions of bacteria that in turn produce waste products that are essential for the formation of soil. Soil in turn churns out vegetables, consumed by those same animals.

Similarly, the line that describes the global value chain of goods and services can be transformed into a circle, where the waste of one process becomes food for another. The "Cradle to Cradle" approach and many other potent concepts have turned companies that have discovered this secret into industry champions. *From line to circle* is the central principle of the Overfished Ocean Strategy, but to make it work, four more "secrets" are essential.

Two: From Vertical to Horizontal

Imagine the global value chain of the industry you're in. This long line consists of many steps: upstream, reaching to your company, and downstream, touching your customers, consumers, and end-of-life entities. This line is also many layers deep, with different industries feeding and interacting with each other. Growing up in business, we are taught to look downstream, paying attention to our customers and consumers. We are asked to pay attention to our immediate suppliers—to make sure that we have secured prices and quantities. But even more so, we are asked to pay utmost attention to the vertical cut in this chain—our competitors.

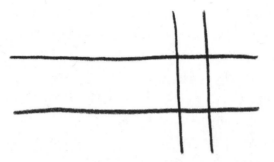

Surely, mainstream strategic thought invites us to pay attention to the whole of five forces in business (competitors, consumers, suppliers, new entrants, and substitutes),[14] but in reality, most dig into the competition, positioning their businesses uniquely in that narrow vertical cut of a global value chain. Yet in the world of rapidly declining resources, this choice might just be the one that kills you—along with the entire competitive space. Surely, you might have the best price or the most unique set of product features, but failure to notice changes far away at the left or the right of the value chain might cause elimination of the entire product line, company, and even industry. We must learn to move *from a vertical to a horizontal* orientation, going beyond the boundaries of our company to the risks—and opportunities— hiding within the entire system.

Three: From Growth to Growth

Ask managers in Atlanta, Delhi, or Copenhagen where their growth comes from, and they will give you a clear answer: selling more. Yet in a world constrained by every type of resource, including landfill space, only one type of "selling more" is possible. We are taught to look at our businesses in terms of our products—even the financial services industry uses the term "product." Yet it is precisely in the service of creating more with less—designing a total solution, a unique experience—where growth lies.

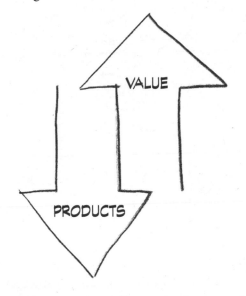

The surprise is that once you sell a total solution, rather than get attached to one specific product, you are eternally motivated to innovate with the highest level of resource intelligence. Once we put aside products and start selling relevance, the question changes. It is not "To grow or not to grow?" but "What do you want to grow?"

Four: From Plan to Model

What do we do when we want to launch something new? How do we turn a hunch, an idea, into a true, commercially successful innovation? The "normal" decades-old path looks something like this: develop a solid, detailed plan (five years seems to be the assumption behind most business plans); get financial backing (budget approval in the existing corporation or investment/loan for a start-up); develop your product to perfection; and sell as much as you can. But for the world of overfished oceans, planning is overrated. In the face of extreme uncertainty, plans become obsolete in no time.

The only way to make the new reality work is to constantly adapt your business to the new reality—treating it as a strategic priority rather than a short-lived sidekick to the core business. For companies mastering the Overfished Ocean Strategy, business modeling, rather than strategic planning, is the name of the game. Unlike cumbersome, static, and rigid plans, models are agile, evolving, and open to change. Modeling, rather than planning, is the key to turning *line to circle*— and making money in the process.

Five: From Department to Mind-Set

Every crisis calls for a hero—a new department, a new VP, a new project manager is born. Unfortunately, when it comes to the fundamental changes in the marketplace driven by the disappearing linear economy, a few "converted" can hardly make a dent in the way that processes, products, and services are developed and delivered. As a result, the hero becomes nothing more than a scapegoat—a poor soul in charge of meaningless glossy reports and pet projects. The new market reality demands a new mind-set, a new way for the entire company to look at the world, rather than a new scapegoat. As this mind-set takes over all functions and all layers of the company hierarchy, you can learn how to discover value where it was previously invisible and impossible.

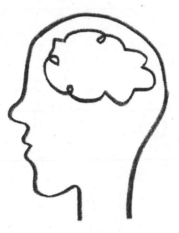

The five big secrets I am laying before you are not meant to be a complete and comprehensive set. Rather, these are a few brushstrokes among the many trends that define the background of the emerging Overfished Ocean Strategy. Together, these five principles pave the way for the emergence of the world that is yet to come—one that takes the line and turns it into a circle, channeling the art of resourcefulness into the world of infinity. In the following chapters, we will explore each of these principles, or disciplines, in depth, traveling through the many companies that have invented their way into the new economic order. Trust me, there is plenty for all of us.

CHAPTER 3

Principle One: Line to Circle

AT A GLANCE

WE ARE RUNNING OUT of things to mine and places to trash.
Why not connect the two ends of the global economy
and turn the line into a circle? Useless waste becomes
a valuable resource that we can circulate indefinitely.
Abundance follows.

"We are allowed to be creative. And in being creative, it allows you to do things differently and find ways you haven't even thought of before. And that type of environment makes it very rewarding, very exciting, to come to work every day." Surrounded by neatly ordered machinery and glassware that could have come straight out of a high school chemistry class, Jeff Wright, senior chemist at Shaw Industries, looks nothing like the messy creative type.[1] With $4 billion in annual sales and 25,000 employees, his company has nothing in common with the infamous start-up garages known for creative vibes. And the product he is talking about can hardly be called sexy: carpet tile.

For decades, old carpeting ended up at landfills. Approximately four billion tons of it gets wasted each year in the United States alone. Like many of the products we use every day, carpet is heavily petro-leum dependent: up to 90 percent of the carpet today is made from synthetic materials, primarily nylon, polypropylene, and polyester. So from the perspective of the disappearing linear economy, the four billion tons wasted each year are pure gold. Well, pure oil, actually. How can we possibly take that gold and use it again—turning a linear economy into a circular one? How do we move *from line to circle*?

If you take a conventional synthetic carpet—like the one you probably have under your feet right now—and slice a knife through it, you will notice that it is built in layers. On top are the soft, plush fibers, made in most cases of nylon, and on the bottom is backing, much of which is made of PVC (polyvinyl chloride). PVC, a product widely used in construction and other industries, has been linked to many controversies. For our purposes, however, only one controversy matters: in the production of carpeting, layers attached to PVC cannot be reused again, making such carpet automatically a one-time-use, throwaway product. But behind the scenes of the carpet mainstream, Shaw Industries developed a groundbreaking carpet backing that would change the company history and push the entire industry toward product infinity. And that happened over a decade ago!

The completely recyclable EcoWorx product hit the market in 1999, premiering at NeoCon, the largest interior design show in the United States. The birth of EcoWorx was a collaboration between divisions at Shaw and partnerships with outside companies, such as Dow Chemical.

"In the mid-1980s, when we first entered the carpet tile business, one of the things we wanted to do was to be able to differentiate ourselves, and we saw an opportunity to do so with a backing system." In our interview video, James Jarrett, director of manufacturing for Commercial Broadloom at Shaw Industries, oozes confidence and firmness through his soft southern accent.

> We went into PVC in the early '90s, and indeed, within five or six years, we've established ourselves as a significant player, and so at that point we were ready to really bring back out some of the ideas around doing something differently, in particular with a thermoplastic type of backing system. We were able to cannibalize parts of some other lines to piece together the EcoWorx line to do the development. And from that point forward, we had the ability to rapidly go through the iterative process of design, trial, and redesign. We spent some long, long months trying to find the right combination of chemistry to make it successful.

The time spent in development was long indeed, but well justified. You see, the traditional PVC products are quite flexible and therefore conform well to the floor. A lot of the products Shaw looked at to replace PVC were very rigid and thus would require a compromise of product quality and performance—a compromise this company was not ready to make. Recyclability *and* performance were necessary. The result of innovation endurance was the EcoWorx backing system, which is lighter and more flexible than traditional high-performance backing, for easier installation and more efficient shipping—all while being 100 percent recyclable. "From 1999, the initial launch, to 2002, so really three years later, the production of both of those backing systems—PVC and EcoWorx—was identical," says Jeff Galloway, director of carpet tile operations. "While I thought it would be 10 or 15 percent of my business, it quickly became 50 percent and growing rapidly. In that time period, we had to retrain our workforce; we had to retool a lot of equipment; we spent around $30 million in this facility phasing out old technology and phasing in the new. We see today it was well worth that investment." Indeed, as of 2013, two-thirds of Fortune 100 companies have EcoWorx products on their floors—among them, Bank of America, Home Depot, Microsoft, and Time Warner.

Steve Bradfield, corporate director for environmental affairs at Eco-Worx, explains the reason for such commercial success: "This was sort of the old-felt need, the holy grail of the carpet tile industry to create a backing that was as good as PVC, and even better than PVC. We did some projections and had a very strong feeling that we could forward-price this at the current market price and take a hit on our profitability during that time, and yet, with an idea that we would swing it the other way very quickly. And that is in fact what happened."

But the riveting revenues are only one side of the story. On the other side is the costs—where once-wasted carpet tile has now become an infinite raw material. The EcoWorx "circular" economy is as simple as it can get. The old carpet tile is taken in, it's ground up, and it goes into the air separator, whereby heavy components fall out as backing and light components get separated out as fiber. Aside from recycled carpet tiles, EcoWorx's backing platform can take in recycled plastic grocery bags and many other similar materials, making this a very robust product.

Naturally, such a simple technology can work only if the collection of used tile is streamlined as well. Jeff Galloway explains:

> Our customers are literally begging for sustainable solutions. They are looking for suppliers like Shaw Industries to come up with technology that is mainstream, that is simple to use. So when we

sell every single square yard of carpet at this facility, it comes with an environmental guarantee, which is: when you are through with it, no matter where, no matter who, call that number—we'll come and pick it up at our expense. For most customers, that is a pretty good deal: I don't have to pay to get it to the landfill; all I have to do is call this number. It is a pretty simple process. From the engineering point of view, it is really exciting to see that process, really neat to think that just within few days of getting a phone call, that old carpet can be made into a new carpet.

Steve Bradfield's words drive the story home:

It's a philosophy of abundance and growth. It's about not being guilty about consumption—if you can create the materials that can stay in perpetual loops. And so, for a businessperson, that is pretty attractive, because it doesn't talk about all the negative aspects of resource scarcity and depletion; it talks about taking technical nutrients made of oil and keeping them in circulation so that we don't deplete all of our resources.[2]

DON'T WORRY ABOUT FAILURE; you only have to be right once.

DREW HOUSTON
FOUNDER AND CEO, DROPBOX

The concept of the circular economy is not new. Throughout the world, companies similar to Shaw are experimenting with solutions similar to EcoWorx in an effort to develop competencies and frameworks necessary to move *from line to circle*. Simply put, the circular economy is "generative by design," as the Ellen MacArthur Foundation puts it: nothing is wasted; everything is going around in a circle.[3] The foundation, which counts major corporations such as Renault, BT, and Cisco among its founding partners, suggests that this simple idea is worth more than $2 trillion to the global economy—no wonder that executives, designers, and consultants alike are jumping on it.[4] Paul Polman, CEO, Unilever, is among them:

> An economy that extracts resources at increasing rates . . . without consideration for our natural planetary boundaries cannot continue indefinitely. In a world of soon to be nine billion consumers . . . , this approach will hamper companies and undermine economies. We need a new way of doing business. The concept of a circular economy promises a way out. Here, products do not quickly become waste, but are reused to extract their maximum value before safely and productively returning to the biosphere. Most importantly for business leaders, such an economy can deliver growth.[5]

And it is all built on a solid, well-tested set of ideas.

The Brief History of the Circle

By any account, moving *from line to circle* is an idea that developed in collaboration spanning decades. As far back as 1966, Kenneth Boulding, one of the most remarkable economists of the 20th century, introduced the idea of circular material flows as a model for the economy in his paper imaginatively titled *The Economics of the Coming Spaceship Earth*. Two unorthodox architects entered into conversation in the late 1970s working independently but thinking very much alike.

In California, John Lyle, a landscape architecture professor, challenged his graduate students at California State Polytechnic University in Pomona to imagine and design a community that ran all of its daily activities within the limits of available renewable resources without any resource repletion or environmental degradation. This simple challenge grew into the concept of *regenerative design*, whereby products and services have infinity built in from the blueprint on. Thirty years of Lyle's work found their home in his 1994 book *Regenerative*

Design for Sustainable Development, which went largely unnoticed by the business community.

Meanwhile, on the other side of the planet, at around the same time, Swiss architect Walter Stahel offered a vision of a closed-loop economy and its impact on job creation, economic competitiveness, resource savings, and waste prevention. Stahel referred to this "closed loop" approach as "Cradle to Cradle" (as opposed to the "cradle to grave" reality of the linear economy)—an expression that stuck. Twenty years later, Stahel built upon his idea further with a rather novel idea: what if we were to sell all goods as services? What if we were not selling shoes but rather renting them? That would ensure control over precious resources put into each shoe, as at the end of the rental agreement the worn shoes would come back ready to be reused. Insisting that this was the most efficient strategy of the circular economy, Stahel described the approach in his 2006 book *The Performance Economy*, illustrating it with hundreds of business examples, but the book didn't make much of a splash within the business community.

Building on Lyle's and Stahel's ideas, German chemist Michael Braungart and American architect William McDonough continued to develop the Cradle to Cradle idea.[6] The result of this collaboration—the 2002 book *Cradle to Cradle: Remaking the Way We Make Things*—put forth a crucial point: considering the way we make things, one circle is simply not enough. In fact, to transform the line productively, we need *two* of them.

Imagine the entire flow of products and services we call "industry" as one giant metabolism—where every resource serves as an important nutrient. Some of these nutrients can be processed and recycled (literally!) by nature itself—where nature would take waste at the end of the use and process it into new resources. We call these types of nutrients *biodegradable*—a term I am sure you are familiar with. Yet human ingenuity produced a number of "nutrients" that nature has a hard time swallowing—it simply does not know what to do with them, requiring hundreds, if not thousands, of years to process them into valuable resources again. For these types of nutrients (remember Shaw's EcoWorx?), humans need to take care of the circulation—processing products at the end of their life into new products. Braungart and McDonough called these two types of nutrients "biological" and "technical," whereby Cradle to Cradle design takes the safe and productive processes of nature's "biological metabolism" as a model for developing a "technical metabolism" flow of industrial materials.

The book—which itself was an example of a "technical" nutrient, as it was made using Durabook technology, whereby the pages are not paper but rather synthetics created from durable, waterproof, and upcyclable plastic resins and inorganic fillers—created quite a stir in industry and academia alike.

And this is when things got interesting.

Ford's $18 Million Roof

The year was 1917, and Ford Motor Company was flying high. Its groundbreaking Model T was in the ninth year of production, delivering affordable travel to the middle class worldwide. It was time to build a new plant. Eleven years later, the completed Ford River Rouge Complex in Dearborn, Michigan, had become the largest integrated factory in the world.

Nearly a century after, William McDonough signed an agreement with Ford Motor Company to redesign this famous 1,212-acre

(490 hectare) Rouge River facility. Among many details of the 1999 proposal, one caused the most hesitation. McDonough proposed to cover the roof of the 1.1-million-square-foot (100,000 square meters) Dearborn truck assembly plant with nothing other than . . . moss. Well, some trees were involved, too.

Met with resistance and dismissal for being such an unusual decoration, the roof was anything but. McDonough explains:

> After lots of discussion and several visits to buildings with green roofs, [Ford's] Jay Richardson's skepticism began to give way. The US Environmental Protection Agency was developing new storm water regulations, and Ford had estimated that the conventional technical controls required to comply with the new rules could cost almost $50 million. The natural storm water management system was estimated to cost only $15 million. The math was simple and compelling: the living roof offered millions of dollars in savings, with the landscape thrown in for free. Kind of gets your attention.[7]

The result? With a final price tag of $18 million, the installed lightweight roof delivered savings of approximately $30 million, compared with the cost of conventional storm water management systems. Over one million square feet of roof got covered with sedum—a low-growing plant—enough to clean up to 20 billion gallons (or about 75 billion liters) of rainwater annually with zero energy, compared with a heavy system requiring its own power supply. Improved biodiversity and landscape in a heavily degraded industrial environment was a welcome bonus, and the roof became a disruptive idea demonstrating the *line-to-circle* principle at work: feeding a healthy nutrient (clean water) back to the soil in the most natural way possible, while at the same time preventing flooding by playing a retention role. No wonder the *New York Times* called it an economic necessity, echoing the words of Bill Ford, then Ford's chief, spoken at the completion of the roof in 2002: "This is not environmental philanthropy. It is sound business."[8]

WASTE EQUALS FOOD, WHETHER it's food for the earth or for a closed industrial cycle. We manufacture products that go from cradle to grave. We want to manufacture them from cradle to cradle.

WILLIAM MCDONOUGH
ARCHITECT AND AUTHOR

Give Me More

Throughout the world, disruptions like EcoWorx's carpet tile backing and Ford's River Rouge living roof make the transition *from line to circle* a bit smoother for the rest of us. Paving the way for a whole new reality, the innovations emerge by the hundreds, solving emergent problems and ironing out strategic wrinkles. The 2010 book *The Blue Economy: 10 Years, 100 Innovations, 100 Million Jobs*, by Gunter Pauli, offers 100 such solutions to choose from. The second edition of *The Performance Economy*, by Walter Stahel, offers a collection of 300 solutions. The Circular Economy 100 and other efforts of the Ellen MacArthur Foundation bring together companies, innovators, and regions to accelerate the transition to a circular economy. The foundation shares a growing list of innovations via its 2012 and 2013 *Towards the Circular Economy* reports, collection of online cases, and other publications. GameStop, the world's largest multichannel video game retailer, is among them.

"If you want to understand GameStop, you must understand refurbishment."[9] This take on corporate identity by the GameStop CEO, Paul Raines, can hardly be called inspirational, but a 182,000-square-foot (around 16,900 square meters) facility filled with workers polishing discs; putting together video game consoles; and scrupulously testing pre-owned iPads, iPhones, iPods, and Android tablets, speaks louder than any words. A 20-employee operation in 2000, 12 years later the Refurbishment Operations Center is a $7 million facility with more than 1,100 professionals working in various functions, such as the giant testing unit, where iPads, iPods, and iPhones are checked for basic functionality of the buttons, the screen, the microphone, the headphone jack, the charging port, and software features. One such station rolls out one tested product every 42 seconds.

Originally a "normal" software and video game retailer, GameStop quickly saw an opportunity in recircling the products that were at the end of their life. As the customers began to move to new electronics more and more quickly, abandoning fully functional products before the end of their life, few companies provided an easy, attractive process for turning wasted electronics into value for consumers. Remember all those old cell phones no longer in use? GameStop took them on, along with a growing list of products in a wide range of electronics. Take Android tablets, for example—the company now accepts 42 different ones for trade-in credit and plans to refurbish and sell all of them before long, as it already sells new Android devices at 1,600 stores. "Why would a retailer have a factory? This was a big bet on the future," says Raines. This bet brought along significant know-how challenges: for every product accepted into the refurbishing cycle, GameStop had to figure out how to reverse engineer it in the most cost-effective way, without any guidance from the manufacturing companies. The result: a growing set of competencies for a new world. Today, GameStop has a strong skill set around buying, selling and trading. "We could trade shoes if we wanted to," says Raines.

And the refurbishing experiment seemed to pass its 2011 experimental stage: in 2012, sales of rebuilt mobile devices alone were projected at $200 million. Products that are hopeless and cannot be refurbished are either dismantled for parts or destroyed and then recycled. More than three million pounds of electronic waste got recycled in 2011. But the plant also does double duty as a manufacturing center and an idea incubator, where the new history is being developed. And the industry seems to agree. In his 2012 article for the *Verge*, Sean Hollister put it best: "Somewhere in here, amidst the shattered screens and broken drive trays, lies the future of retail."[10]

The recent (and never-ending) economic crisis left many companies struggling with overcapacity. Business equipment, skills and knowledge of employees, and real estate all stood still as sales plummeted and the flow of goods and services stalled. Four years after Lehman Brothers' bankruptcy, volumes have been recovering slowly, but the overcapacity remains. FLOOW2 looked at this omnipresent challenge as a glowing business opportunity and became the first business-to-business marketplace to enable companies and institutions to share equipment and personnel skills that are currently underutilized.[11] The platform was launched in early 2012, and one year later it was offering over 4,500 types of equipment and services.

The company's business model is based on the concept of collaborative consumption, where participants share access to products or services, rather than pursue individual ownership. FLOOW2 took a well-tested peer-to-peer and end-consumer model (after all, it has been successful in such areas as peer-to-peer accommodation [Airbnb], peer-to-peer task assignments [TaskRabbit], and car sharing [Zipcar])—and applied it to a business-to-business sector. The natural starting point for the company was the heavy-equipment market, but they went out of the comfort zone, detecting a number of other, less obvious markets in which the platform could trade overcapacity, among them health care, knowledge and skills, transport and logistics, and theater and events.

No question, user-friendliness is the key to the success of FLOOW2. For customers, the process starts with easy and free registration—if you have some capacity to share, you have simple ways of posting what is available and when; and different forms of insurance and assurances exist to protect all parties. The company developed the customer interface of their platform to include a free online planning tool for managing equipment requirements and availability. They also provide additional services, such as online payment services, credit checks, tracking and trace service on assets, and insurance through partnerships with other businesses. And the revenue is generated through fees that participants pay to advertise their equipment on the platform, at a cost of EUR €1 (approximately $1.30 US) per day as well as by subscription.

While they were disturbed and disrupted at first, "FLOOW2 is noticing that professional renting companies, OEMs [original equipment manufacturers], and leasing companies accept that collaborative use is here to stay," note Will Robben, company founder, and Geraldine Brennan, doctoral researcher, Imperial College London.

Trendwatching.com called this phenomenon "owner-less," adding it to its "11 Crucial Consumer Trends for 2011." The reasons seem rather clear:

- Traditional ownership implies a certain level of responsibility, cost, and commitment. Consumers looking for convenience and collecting as many experiences as possible want none of these things.

- Fractional ownership and leasing lifestyle businesses offer the possibility of perpetual upgrades to the latest and greatest, the ability to maximize the number and variety of experiences, and allow consumers to access otherwise out-of-reach luxuries.

- Owning bulky, irregularly used items is both expensive and unsustainable, especially in dense urban environments where space is at a premium. With more consumers having mobile access to online systems, it becomes easier to book items whenever and wherever they are needed.[12]

No wonder *Time* magazine named collaborative consumption among its 2010 "10 Ideas That Will Change the World."[13] CNBC estimates that companies that provide access—rather than ownership—could generate $3.5 billion in 2013. Among them are Uber and Airbnb—numbers 6 and 12, respectively, on the *Fast Company* list of the World's 50 Most Innovative Companies in 2013.

Uber, a geo-tracking app that makes private cars and drivers available at any time to registered users in a matter of minutes, has grown its operations to 21 cities worldwide as of 2013. The value proposition for the consumer is rather obvious: get a clean car, a professional driver, and automatic billing (no cash necessary)—all at your fingertips. In 2012, the company reported growing more than 20 percent month over month. "The company's CEO and founder, Travis Kalanick, said the straightforward consumer experience of pushing a button so 'a Mercedes pulls up' provides better ways for urban dwellers to navigate transportation," said CNBC.[14]

Airbnb, the poster child of the sharing economy, grew out of the same idea: you have a spare room in your apartment or a tree house suitable for adventurous traveler—we will let you rent it out! Founded in 2008, the company now offers stays in over 34,000 cities in 192 countries, with over 10 million nights booked by the end of 2012. As expected, the company battles a number of problems associated with an innovative business model—including the issue of paying taxes on the money paid to the individuals or meeting the housing code requirements. Yet the venture seems to push through all of them in stride. "This year, Airbnb is moving beyond rentals to partner with local communities and enhance the entire travel experience," says Lindsay Harrison of *Fast Company*. "Our product isn't just our website; it's also our hosts, listings, users, photographers, and employees. Our product is the entire community," echoes Brian Chesky, company CEO. I am sold.

NO MATTER THE PHRASING—sharing economy, connected economy, collaborative consumption—20- and 30-something entrepreneurs expanding consumers' access and experienced veterans agree that offering a new path to consumer purchases means lasting or possibly revolutionary change to the way we experience commerce, increasing the importance of both trust in transactions and easy technology.

KATIE KRAMER
PRODUCER, "ON THE MONEY," CNBC

From Line to Circle: The Practicalities

Making the transition *from line to circle* is a daunting task, but the elephant does not need to be eaten in one bite. The good news is that the past decade offered ample opportunities for experimentation, and thousands of companies went through a trial-and-error process to figure out how to make it happen. Three simple and well-known options are available for consideration:

- Reuse

- Refurbish

- Recycle

Reuse has been around for a long time. The key to reusing your waste with a real financial bang is to explore opportunities beyond the obvious. Collaborative consumption tales of FLOOW2, Uber, and Airbnb are examples of such creative sharing, but there is another way of looking it. A recent McKinsey & Company report, for example, suggests betting on the power of "cascaded use"—whereby reuse is spread across many different industries in the value chain, such as "when cotton clothing is reused first as second-hand apparel, then crosses to the furniture industry as fiber-fill in upholstery, and the fiber-fill is later reused in stone wool insulation for construction—in each case substituting for an inflow of virgin materials into the economy—before the cotton fibers are safely returned to the biosphere."[15]

Another way of taking the reuse idea to the next level is through what is known as the model of *industrial symbiosis*, in which by-products of one industrial process can become a valuable raw material for another. In manufacturing, for example, steam produced in one factory can be sold to another plant nearby. The best-known example of industrial symbiosis is located in Kalundborg, Denmark, where seven companies reuse each other's by-products or residuals from production on a commercial basis, including energy cooperation, water cooperation, and by-product cooperation. Here is one example: More than 98 percent of the sulfur in the flue gas from the Asnæs Power Station is removed before it leaves the plant, and then it gets reused by the plasterboard manufacturer Gyproc as a substitute for imported gypsum. The symbiosis reduced CO_2 emissions by 265,000 tons annually, which would be equivalent to annual emissions from electricity use of about 80,000 single-family houses. The symbiosis reduces water use by 30 percent, while 100,000 tons of gypsum are salvaged from the flue gas desulphurization each year.[16]

But it is the service industry where the innovation has boomed recently. (This one is for all of you working in services and having trouble discovering your Overfished Ocean Strategy!) And one service industry powers up all the others: IT. "Cloud computing is hot, literally. Electricity consumed by computers and other IT equipment has been skyrocketing in recent years, and has become a substantial part of the global energy market. In 2006, the IT industry used 61 billion kWh electricity (or 3% of total energy consumption in the United States), and is the fastest growing industrial sector"—that was a starting point for a group of Microsoft researchers backed by the Computer Science Department of the University of Virginia.[17] The remarkable thing is that all the millions spent on electricity used to power up data servers gets converted into heat—so IT professionals have to spend millions on electricity to power up the air conditioning systems needed to cool them off! That is one wasteful process. The solution to the growing resource trouble? Use the data servers as furnaces to heat homes.

> Physically, a computer server is a metal box that converts electricity into heat. The temperature of the exhaust air (usually around 40°–50°C) is too low to regenerate electricity efficiently, but is perfect for heating purposes, including home/building space heating, clothes dryers, water heaters, and agriculture. We propose to replace electric resistive heating elements with silicon heating elements, thereby reducing the societal energy footprint by using electricity for heating to also perform computation. . . . Home heating alone constitutes about 6% of the US energy usage. By piggy-backing on only half of this energy, the IT industry could double in size without increasing its carbon footprint or its load on the power grid and generation systems.[18]

While Microsoft's efforts are still in the research stage, the direction of their thinking is groundbreaking, perhaps even disorienting. The invitation to all of us is loud and clear: it's time to take reuse to another level!

Refurbishing (replacing one or a few parts of a used or broken product) and remanufacturing (completely overhauling the used product, restoring it to a new condition) offer another opportunity for value creation—by restoring the product to nearly its original state. The key to refurbishing and remanufacturing success is finding a cost-effective and consumer-friendly process for collecting the product you wish to work with. GameStop collects its wide range of electronics to be refurbished at a handful of collection centers, but its own retail chain makes this easy. Shaw provides a toll-free number for customers to call, and they pick up anything more than 500 yards of carpet. TerraCycle, the worm-poop fertilizer company we visited in chapter 1, has come up with an even more innovative collection system, as it creates a significant value for the collectors well beyond a traditional financial return.

The company uses soda bottles, juice pouches, and hundreds of other nonrecyclable or hard-to-recycle waste items and turns them into backpacks, picture frames, clipboards, and a wide range of other products that are sold at Walmart, Target, and many other outlets. To collect the magnificent diversity of raw material, TerraCycle created a unique fundraising opportunity, whereby schools, churches, and other organizations earn money for valuable social causes, all while keeping tons of waste out of the landfill. As of mid-2013, more than 36,041,000 people had collected more than 2,508,577,000 units of waste (yes, that is in billions!), generating more than $5,685,000 for charitable causes.[19]

HP, which transformed refurbishing into a wide-ranging global offering called Renew that provides "nearly twice the hardware for the price," uses a trade-in program for the collection of its "raw material."[20] Customers follow a simple online process to get a free quote for the product they would like to sell back. If the quote is attractive, the participant can get new HP products in return and receive cash back for what is left over. Collect and prosper!

———————

Recycling requires a completely different level of complexity, whereby the product is broken down into incomprehensibly small parts and the resulting raw material is sold into an often-different industry. In the world of overfished oceans, recycling seems to be the hottest business idea around. Just a second ago, my simple Google search for "start recycling business" produced 59,700,000 results, offering in-depth why and how manuals on starting your own recycling company. The reason for this is clear: it's an opportunity for strong growth. Frost and Sullivan, a consulting company specializing in growth, estimates that recycling services alone will more than double in market size from $158 billion in 2011 to $322 billion in 2017.[21]

Recycling is the best-known way of turning trash into cash. However, most innovative companies find a way to generate additional value through their recycling activities, aside from the financial benefit of the raw-material recovery. In 2007, Coca-Cola took on one of its many reputational risks—plastic bottles—and recycled them into $15 million in sales. Drink2Wear T-shirts were made from recycled plastic bottles (much like fleece and other apparel you own that already contains recycled bottles) blended with cotton and featured slogans such as "Make Your Plastic Fantastic" and "Rehash Your Trash."[22] The T-shirts became so popular that in 2008, Coke expanded its product portfolio to include totes, loungewear, and caps. The products appeared in more than 1,500 stores throughout the United States—promoting recycling to the customers, fostering a positive brand image for the company, and creating value from previously trashed raw material, all at the same time. As of 2012, Coca-Cola had sold more than one million Drink2Wear units, bringing in more than $15 million in retail sales. Recycle, please.

Building Your Tool Kit

Moving *from line to circle* is the foundational, cornerstone principle for all businesses pursuing the Overfished Ocean Strategy. Yet it is understandable that such fundamental transformation does not happen overnight. As a metaphor, I often compare this tenacious process to the complexity of transforming a working, plugged-in TV set into a working, plugged-in vacuum cleaner—without any disturbance to the service. Oh my!

Here are a few *line-to-circle* resources that you might consider for your emerging Overfished Ocean Strategy tool kit:

- *Cradle to Cradle: Remaking the Way We Make Things*, by William McDonough and Michael Braungart (New York: North Point Press, 2002), has a loyal following by business, academia, and public leaders alike—an easy and potent read. Since its release, the ideas grew into a full-blown movement, and you should be able to find a community of Cradle to Cradle practitioners nearby. One place to start exploring the resources is the website of the Cradle to Cradle Products Innovation Institute: http://c2ccertified.org/.

- The Ellen MacArthur Foundation, which I refer to constantly, is not your ordinary charity but rather a new community of business leaders all dedicated to the idea of the circular economy. On its site, you will find excellent reports managed and analyzed by McKinsey & Company, case studies, courses, visuals, and more. The videos and visuals can be valuable as conversation starters at management meetings: they are precise, business focused, and to the point. Make sure to visit the foundation's site often: http://www.ellenmacarthurfoundation.org/.

- Blue Economy (or Green Economy 2.0, as they often call themselves) is another excellent resource working within the *line-to-circle* philosophy. The site will challenge you with completely new ideas (such as gravity as an alternative energy source) and give you access to success stories of businesses making it work: http://www .blueeconomy.eu/ (English version).

- *Biomimicry: Innovation Inspired by Nature*, by Janine M. Benyus (New York: William Morrow, 1997; Kindle ed., 2009), became the loud voice of the biomimicry movement. The idea is simple: Nature has already figured out how to solve many of our most complex problems, so why don't we mimic biology to make it all work? Spiders have developed a weaving technology of amazing strength (compare the web's net weight with that of the captured fly!), so why not apply that to textiles? How about calcium buildup, which plumbers have fought for generations? Marine creatures that live in shells figured out that problem as well, so why not borrow their solutions? Considering the fact that the circular economy itself mimics nature, you might find this school of thought refreshing. The Biomimicry 3.8 website is a good place to start: http://biomimicry.net/.

- The resilience movement is another source of good tools and ideas. One hub within this movement is the Center for Resilience at Ohio State University. The center developed a number of cool tools, among them software that allows you to map out by-product synergies and thus turn your waste into profits. You can find out a lot more at the center's website: http://resilience.osu.edu/.

———

From line to circle is the first of five key principles that make the Overfished Ocean Strategy work. It is a fundamental shift in the way you do business—the most important shift needed to survive and thrive in the resource-deprived world. Yet it is not enough. You also need to go *from vertical to horizontal*. The next chapter shows how.

CHAPTER 4

Principle Two: Vertical to Horizontal

AT A GLANCE

WE ARE TAUGHT TO look nearby—to our customers, competition, and suppliers—for sources of unique competitive advantage. Yet in the world of overfished oceans, risks and opportunities are hiding far away from the home grounds—among the suppliers of the suppliers of the suppliers, and customers of customers of customers. Expand your horizons.

We started this journey with a broad, bird's-eye look at our global economy—the linear throwaway economy, to be precise. Now it's time to take a much closer look—at each individual strand, each individual industry that plays a role within the complex weave that is our market.

Take your industry, for example. The global value chain of your industry can be drawn out as a line, consisting of many stages and companies—upstream through all the suppliers, reaching to your company, and downstream, touching your customers, consumers, and end-of-life enterprises. Growing up in business, we are taught to look downstream from our business, paying attention to our customers and consumers (the customer is king, right?). We are also naturally tracking the flow upstream leading to our company—suppliers can make or break our profit margin. But more than anything, we are asked to pay our utmost attention to the *vertical* cut in this chain: our competitors.

Surely, mainstream strategic thought invites us to pay attention to the whole of five forces in business (competitors, consumers, suppliers, new entrants, and substitutes).[1] But in reality, most managers dig into the competition, searching for a sweet spot for their businesses in that *vertical* cut of a global value chain.

And that might just be the thing that kills you—along with the entire competitive space.

Let me illustrate. If your company is Apple, when it comes to producing computers, in addition to customer needs, you are trained to look at your direct competitors, such as Sony, Dell, and many others. You are also invited to explore your strategic options by looking at substitute products and the most powerful suppliers. It is, however, very unlikely that as a part of your normal strategic thinking you are conditioned to look routinely into what is happening far and away in the global value chain—say, explore what is going on with tomato farms in Vietnam (I am, of course, just using this as an illustration). Yet it could well be one spot where future risk—and opportunity—hides.

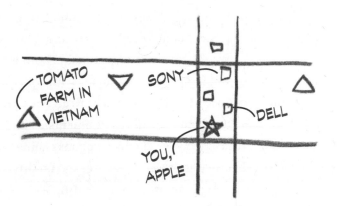

In the world of rapidly declining resources and subsequent growing demands, the *vertical* orientation is a handicap to leave behind—
fast. Surely, you might have the best price or the most unique, most
unexpected combination of product features, but the failure to notice
changes far away on the left or the right of the value chain might cause
elimination of the entire product line, company, and even industry.
Companies that have mastered the Overfished Ocean Strategy made
the move *from a vertical to a horizontal* orientation, going beyond the
safe boundaries of their companies to the risks—and opportunities—
hiding within the entire system. And that is not an easy transition.

———————

The coffee industry discovered the power of *horizontal* thinking
the hard way. Until the 1990s, much of the coffee supply was regu-
lated, with prices and quotas closely guarded by a series of International Coffee Agreements. Then, with changes in the political winds,
most coffee-producing countries liberalized their coffee industries,
letting the market forces run wild. On the other side of the supply
chain, coffee-consuming countries were changing as well. Starbucks,

which was founded in 1971, grew well beyond its humble roots, opening an average of two new stores a day between 1987 and 2007.[2] On the heels of this giant, Dunkin' Donuts and McDonald's both worked on their offerings, along with a range of new chains with coffee at the core of their menus. Huge food producers such as Kraft Foods reigned supreme in grocery stores and other retail environments. With their scale and thus their purchasing power, the humongous chains, being the good competitors that they are, relentlessly worked on driving the price of coffee down, engaging in nonstop price-cutting wars. And boy, did they succeed!

Apart from two short-lived price spikes in 1995 and 1997, brought about by the loss of the Brazilian crop to frost, coffee prices have plummeted to the lowest levels recorded in the past 30 years. Adjusted for inflation, the price points in this period have been the lowest in the past 100 years—dropping in 2001 to their historical minimum of just 30 cents per pound for the robusta variety and 60 cents per pound for arabica.[3] For coffee roasters and retailers, what a victory to celebrate!

Not so fast. Much of the coffee is grown by small farms selling their crop through cooperatives—a highly distributed supply system. It takes about five years for a coffee tree to reach the productive stage, which lasts about four additional years. Moreover, there is an inverse relationship between the quality of a coffee bean and the quantity of coffee that the plant can produce. Plants that produce high-quality coffee usually do not produce many beans. Eduardo Ambrocio, who serves the Guatemalan National Coffee Association as a master cupper and quality control expert, puts it this way: "Coffee is a lot like grapes and many other fruits. We have varieties that probably give you a good yield at times of production, but low quality. As a farmer, you are going to focus on either high quantity or high quality."[4]

As the prices of coffee dropped, farmers around the world growing high-quality beans started leaving their vocation by the thousands, abandoning the trees in search of a better living for their families and communities. Because they were independent farmers, their flight was not immediately noticed by their partners upstream until it became a struggle to consistently secure good-quality beans in sufficient quantities. And with a long tree-growing cycle, filling in the gap was not so easy. Suddenly, the entire coffee-roasting industry was threatened.

PART OF WHAT YOU need to do in the supply chain is to help your company anticipate events and understand the environment you operate in—physical, political, economic—around the globe.

> FRANCES TOWNSEND
> CNN CONTRIBUTOR AND
> FORMER HOMELAND SECURITY ADVISER

Learning from the coffee crisis, different companies took different paths toward securing their supply chains. In the premium roast category, for the longest time businesses have focused most of their efforts on differentiating themselves from the competition through a variety of unique roasts or strong brand identity. Clearly, the security of the supply chain was not that high on the list of competitive advantages. Now, this all had to change.

For Green Mountain Coffee Roasters, a publicly traded company founded in Waterbury, Vermont, during the height of coffee prices in 1981, the security of the supply chain became a source of real differentiation. For years, the company competed in the specialty coffee segment, crafting unique roasts from the highest-quality coffee beans. Understanding that there was no other option but to address this exploding risk, the company went through a reengineering of its supply-chain relationships and made the new relationships a core part of its brand identity. When I first encountered the company in 2003, it could boast of being the largest double-certified organic and fair-trade coffee roaster in the world—known for paying its suppliers a price set far above the market average set by a third party. The difference was used by the local coffee growers to secure a normal livelihood, including education and health opportunities, while the company's badges of honor—certification—ensured a cozy share of the growing organic foods market and allowed it to distinguish itself from many other producers on the shelves of the Whole Foods Market and the like.

Today, the company has developed a comprehensive supply-chain resilience strategy. Here is how Green Mountain Coffee Roasters defines it: "Resilience, at its most basic level, refers to an ability to adapt quickly to, or recover from, changes. To GMCR, building a resilient supply chain means helping the producers and manufacturers in our supply chain, as well as their employees and wider communities, to adapt to the many challenges they face and to prosper over the short term and the long term."[5] And the strategy seemed to rub off on the company's financial performance. In 2009, the company was ranked 11th on the *Fortune* 100 Fastest Growing Companies list. For 2012, the latest year for which I have data, Green Mountain reported a 40 percent year-over-year growth in net sales and 82 percent growth in net income—that is resilience, I'd say.[6]

———————

Using horizontal thinking to drive new *revenues* is not the only way to turn supply-chain security into new value. For Portland Roasting Company, redesign of its value-chain relationships became a significant source of *cost savings*. Facing the same supply-security challenge as the rest of the industry, the company toyed with the idea of third-party certification—including fair trade, organic, Rainforest Alliance, Bird Friendly, and many others—and decided that the hefty cost of the certification process did not make sense for a company that sold heavily through HORECA (hotels, restaurants, and cafés) channels and thus had relatively little direct communication with the end consumer. Plus, if the company were to pursue retail distribution, it would be rather hard to compete with the big names playing in the certification field. Walmart launched six eco-friendly and ethical coffees under the Sam's Choice brand. Whole Foods sold its 365 brand of coffee, promoted for its fair-trade practices and direct relationships with more than 40 growers, while Kraft General Foods advertised that 30 percent of all the coffee beans that went into Yuban coffee were officially certified by the Rainforest Alliance. The branding game seemed to have too many players. So instead, Portland Roasting Company decided to pass on that cash directly to the suppliers and created its own supply-chain security program, Farm Friendly Direct, which pays more than fair-trade prices to farmers and cooperatives. Founded in 2001 at the La Hilda Estate in Costa Rica, the program evolved by 2010 to include direct trade arrangements with farmers in Tanzania, El Salvador, Costa Rica, Indonesia, India, Papua New Guinea, Guatemala, and Ethiopia. So why such generosity?

Going directly to the coffee farmers allows for elimination of costly brokers and other supply-chain steps, providing a financial cushion—an opportunity for investment. Because it is a specialty coffee company, quality is at the center of Portland Roasting Company's competitive advantage. Much of the final quality of the product depends on the conditions of harvest, milling, and storage. Coffee may leave the processing mill at the ideal 12 percent moisture content, but if it isn't handled right, quality plummets.[7] Humidity is a critical variable: if coffee absorbs too much moisture, especially from exposure to humid environments when stored for long periods of time, its flavor may take on a moldy overtone. Working directly with the farmers allowed the company to have increased quality control at a decreased cost—and avoid the risk of poor quality stemming from long journeys through brokers' hands. For Portland Roasting Company, that simply made sense.

———————

The pioneering companies of the coffee industry have found a way to transform resource scarcity into a real competitive edge. But they also were very lucky: the coffee crisis of the 1990s served as an excellent catalyst, pushing the entire industry into innovation mode. Most of our industries, however, are not so lucky, and working with suppliers way downstream or customers upstream in the value chain is not an easy task.

WE ALL HAVE PROBABLY spent too much time thinking about "smart individuals." That's one of the problems with schools. They are very individualistic, very much about "the smart kids and the dumb kids." That's not the kind of smartness we need.

The smartness we need is collective. We need cities that work differently. We need industrial sectors that work differently. We need value chains and supply chains that are managed from the beginning until the end to purely produce social, ecological, and economic well-being. That is the concept of intelligence we need, and it will never be achieved by a handful of smart individuals.

It's not about "the smartest guys in the room." It's about what we can do collectively. So the intelligence that matters is collective intelligence, and that's the concept of "smart" that I think will really tell the tale.

PETER SENGE
SCIENTIST, AUTHOR, AND DIRECTOR OF THE
CENTER FOR ORGANIZATIONAL LEARNING AT
THE MIT SLOAN SCHOOL OF MANAGEMENT

Innovation at the Scale of the Whole:
The Curious Case of Fairmount Minerals

"Not since the days of the Great Depression has there been such a severe decline of public trust in business and in our economic system— nor has there been a better opportunity to build a new era of business-led excellence and leadership in our industry and beyond." With her strong words and animated gestures, Jenniffer Deckard looked every inch the CFO of a major mining company—the role she had held for many years. But the audience she was addressing was anything but straightforward. The year was 2005, and for the first time ever, Fair-mount, then a $300 million company and the third-largest producer of industrial sand in the United States, decided to bring together customers, suppliers, employees, NGOs (nongovernmental organizations), local community leaders, and many other stakeholders to collaboratively chart out the new survival strategy.

In the face of increasing resource scarcity and growing pressures from legislators, communities, and the media, mining companies faced greater challenges in winning bids for new mines—obtaining licenses to operate from the local community. When a few hundred participants at the strategic summit came face-to-face, few of them were sure that such an unconventional way to approach strategy had any merit at all. But for the company, this seemed to be the most efficient and productive way to address this big chunk of its value chain at once—and discover new value potential along the way.

And productive it was! The multistakeholder summit resulted in a number of innovation initiatives. Among them was the idea to engage 850 additional stakeholders—customers, neighboring farm-ers, suppliers, and more—in finding new solutions for growing challenges. New minds working on old problems brought about unusual results. One of them was an accidental *line-to-circle* discovery. Chuck Fowler, then CEO and now chairman of Fairmount Minerals, sat down with me for a video interview to share one of many innovation stories stemming from the 2005 launch: "We use a Caterpillar in-loader in our quarries to get the sand through the process. When we finish with processing, we send that sand to Caterpillar, and they produce a core, which makes up the inside dimensions of the castings that are needed to make the engine blocks for a tractor. Once the castings are produced, the sand comes back as 'spent' sand in the foundry." Chuck, whom I've had the pleasure of working with for many years, picked up two differently colored dishes of sand, examples of sand that is beautifully white at the beginning of the process and nearly dark when it's spent. "We've got an excellent process where we take this spent sand, and it goes back to the farmers to spread on the fields, producing higher yields of corn, and that corn gets sold to a company that makes ethanol and biodiesel. We use the biodiesel at our plants for Caterpillar's in-loaders." Without deep engagement of a wide range of stakeholders along the entire horizon of the Fairmount Minerals value chain—upstream and downstream—the idea of reselling the spent sand and closing the loop would never have come about. So how did it happen, exactly?

"During the summit, an engineer in one group shared how spent sand, when placed on farmland, has been shown to help grow higher yields of biomass. Another person declared that the company's sand-mining facilities are located in rural locations near many farms. Between the two observations, a light bulb goes off. How might we create a new business for spent sand? Why not create a new partnership with farmers—a partnership where sand-assisted biomass growth becomes the basis for lower-cost, green biofuels to power the heavy truck fleet," reports 2012 research led by David Cooperrider of Case Western Reserve University and Michelle McQuaid of the University of Melbourne.[8]

The company now uses the multistakeholder whole-system approach when bidding for new mines. In 2006, Fairmount set its sights on a potential mine in Wisconsin and engaged stakeholders in the community in a discussion about coplanning mine operations—well before making the bid. When the town of Tainter selected it over a larger competitor seen as less agile, whole system, and sustainable, the local newspaper published a telling story titled "The Tale of Two Sand Companies." Going way beyond mere compliance in mining operations made all the difference in the company's ability to get preferential access to new strategic assets.

The financial side of the story speaks even louder. Between 2005 and 2007, Fairmount Minerals' revenues from the new "resource intelligent" products almost doubled, while earnings from growth and operational efficiencies took a colossal leap of more than 40 percent per year.[9]

Jenniffer Deckard, who championed the *vertical-to-horizontal* transition in the company with great support from Chuck Fowler, then Fairmount Minerals' president and CEO, and Bill Conway, the company's founder and chairman, speaks to the benefit of a company's widening its horizons this way: "Today's customers, supply-chain partners, community leaders, and employees want to be engaged in a radically new way. Now, I realize that it is not a pipe dream to manage important targets as a whole system—in fact, it's fast. I call it my management macro-moment."[10] In May 2013, Jenniffer succeeded Chuck as company president and CEO.

––––––––

While some companies find the transition *from vertical to horizontal* innovation a bit daunting, others seem to be born right into it. Indeed, most of us find it hard to move from function to function *within* the same company (remember the usual wars between sales and production, or product developers and the finance department?). Horizontal thinking demands that we move far beyond the functional or organizational divide within a company and look for value hidden *between* the companies. A few start-ups are finding success by building on outstanding experiments in the very competence that our businesses and business schools find so foreign and cumbersome. Meet one of them.

Sourcemap: Crowdsourcing on Steroids

"People have a right to know where products come from, what they're made of, and how they impact people and the environment. Sourcemap is the first crowdsourced directory of supply chains and environmental footprints. Join a vibrant community of individuals, businesses, and NGOs using Sourcemap to share information about how things are made." This is the first thing that Sourcemap's website says about the company.[11]

As I type these words, my auto-correct is highlighting the word *crowdsourced* with bright red squiggles, suggesting that this word is not yet part of everyone's vocabulary, so I'd better give a short definition. The practice of crowdsourcing (which was coined in 2006 by editors at *Wired* magazine[12]) means, simply put, sourcing your ideas for products, processes, or solutions from a big crowd—often making an open call for contributions online—rather than the usual small number of employees or suppliers.

While the word is new, the practice is well tested. The Oxford English Dictionary is one of the earliest examples of crowdsourcing. An open call was made for volunteers to help identify all the words in the English language and provide real-life examples of their use for each one. Over a period of 70 years, more than six million submissions were received. Wikipedia is the modern take on this process. Sourcemap works about the same way.

Originally a nonprofit venture, Sourcemap grew into a for-profit enterprise against all odds. Leonardo Bonanni, company CEO, told the story in an extensive *Forbes* interview:

Products are incredibly complex. . . . In the past it was almost impossible to know where a product came from, but that has changed with the advent of the Web, new mapping and satellite techniques, crowd sourcing and social networking. . . . About five years ago I set out to solve the problem of finding out where things come from. It turns out the way to do it is very much like Wikipedia or YouTube, which is to allow everybody to contribute to the collective intelligence. . . . Sourcemap was the first crowd-sourced directory for finding out where things come from and measuring the associated cost.[13]

That is when I learned about Sourcemap—a Robin Hood kind of venture exposing the dirty deeds of industry. In 2010, it took me barely five seconds to discover, for instance, where IKEA's Sultan Alsarp bed comes from, and what kind of environmental impact its ingredients have made along the way. In a matter of a few clicks, I learned that in the making of one bed, 10 kilos of Polish-made indoor plywood are used, with 130.28 kg of CO_2 embedded in plywood production. Galvanized steel from Russia (39.84 kg of CO_2), epoxy resin from China (0.25 kg of CO_2), hydraulics from Germany (4.02 kg of CO_2)—the list was long. None of it was approved by IKEA—and if I were representing the global giant of affordable design furniture, having all this information on display would not make me feel at ease.

Yet surprisingly, companies big and small thought differently. The 2007 nonprofit experiment of the MIT Media Lab went for-profit in April 2011. "The reason for the spinoff from MIT was companies were coming to me and asking if we could help them see what their sourcing maps looked like. The demand from industry has been huge," Bonanni explained. Companies that decide to increase the level of transparency in communicating with clients, suppliers, government, media, and all other stakeholders create an account with Sourcemap.com. Then, they get a chance to upload and share information about their suppliers and publish it for all the world to see—and thus get greater trust in the products sold. The increasing frequency of crises of every

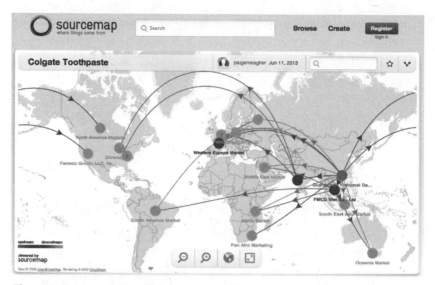

Figure 3. Sourcemap.com helps everyone figure out where things come from—and how to better organize their supply chain. Here is the Colgate Toothpaste supply-chain map created by user paigemeagher.
Source: http://free.sourcemap.com/.

kind—whether it is a volcanic eruption, a tsunami, or an oil spill—has also been driving businesses to find a place where they can see the full picture of the supply chain and see what can be affected and how to manage this risk.[14]

If you are Colgate, the map for toothpaste you are producing might look like the one in Figure 3 that I copied from my screen a minute ago.

Sourcemap took an unrecognized but very real need and turned it into a viable business model—selling subscriptions to its services for $1,000–$10,000 a month to a range of companies, "including EADS and Office Depot, to help them communicate with their suppliers and calculate the risk operations could be disrupted," *Bloomberg Businessweek* reports, awarding Sourcemap a proud place on its "America's Most Promising Social Entrepreneurs 2012" list.[15] The company secured $100,000 in revenues in the first four months of operations.

Building Your Tool Kit

The transition *from vertical to horizontal* is, perhaps, the most difficult, cumbersome, and demanding principle of the Overfished Ocean Strategy. For more than a century, we have been taught to treat business as a conveyor: divide labor, focus on specific functions, master your competition, build high walls protecting your company. As the linear economy gives way to the circular one, the only way to make it work well is to start by understanding—and working—across the entire line. The good news is that a number of great *vertical to horizontal* resources have already been developed and mastered to serve you as you build your own Overfished Ocean Strategy tool kit:

- Appreciative Inquiry is a philosophy of change at the *scale of the whole*—engaging partners up, down, and all around the stream to transform together with your company. Developed by David Cooperrider, Ron Fry, and Suresh Srivastva at Case Western Reserve University, this is exactly the approach that Fairmount Minerals (along with Walmart, Green Mountain Coffee Roasters, and many others) has been using in its multistakeholder strategic-change efforts. A number of unique principles ensure that the adversarial positions that stakeholders bring to the table are transformed into fuel for disruptive innovation—like the spent-sand discovery of Fairmount Minerals. The art of Appreciative Inquiry has been polished for more than 20 years, and the approach has been hailed as the most important innovation in organizational development of the last several decades. And a bonus: instead of protecting the know-how, the creators of Appreciative Inquiry decided to make it "open source," sharing endless amounts of resources for the world to use. You can find these resources in a global online depository at Appreciative Inquiry Commons: http://appreciativeinquiry.case.edu/.

- Many companies have developed comprehensive approaches to *managing the risks* hidden in the supply chain, thus having data to transform such risks into opportunities. Most such approaches include a scorecard for all suppliers. In recent years, I myself have had to fill out countless forms contributing to scorecards of companies large and small in a wide range of industries, including none other than a missile company! Yet with an abundance of scorecards comes an abundance of data, which is often hard to make sense of. To aid with this challenge, the Sustainability Accounting Standards Board (SASB) developed an approach that aids companies in assessing how *material* (read important) particular risks are and which risk might have the most profound impact on the company's ability to create shareholder value. By 2013, SASB created Materiality Maps for 88 industries in 10 sectors. Each map works with 43 different environmental, social, and government issues, ranking the materiality of each issue for a particular industry. A perfect way to start with SASB's Materiality Maps is an article in the *Harvard Business Review* by Robert G. Eccles and George Serafeim titled "The Performance Frontier: Innovating for a Sustainable Strategy."[16]

- The discipline of *systems thinking* has developed a diverse set of tools that allow you to understand the elements of a system and the relationships between them—your own value chain being one such system. While "feedback loops" and "system archetypes" may appear complicated at first, these terms for analyzing and depicting the whole system become incredibly handy when you are discovering the mechanism for disruptive innovation across the life cycle of your product. One classic book has made the discipline of systems thinking accessible to business: *Fifth Discipline: The Art and Practice of the Learning Organization*, by Peter M. Senge (New York: Currency Doubleday, 1990), has been enlightening businesspeople around the world since it was first released in 1990, but it seems more relevant today than ever before. A very easy and practical read on its own, the book was followed up by *The Fifth Discipline Fieldbook: Strategies and Tools for Building a Learning Organization*, by Peter M. Senge, Art Kleiner, Charlotte Roberts, Richard B. Ross, and Bryan J. Smith (New York: Crown Business, 1994), featuring many real-life stories of making systems thinking work at the scale of the whole.

• *Open innovation* is a close relative of the concept of crowdsourcing that we visited in this chapter, but it offers a broader view, championed by Henry William Chesbrough, author of *Open Innovation: The New Imperative for Creating and Profiting from Technology* (Boston: Harvard Business School Press, 2006), along with a number of other books and articles, and professor at the University of California, Berkeley. When it comes to innovation, most companies take a protective stance, guarding it with all their might (and all the might of patent law). The realities of the global transition toward the circular economy are so complex that no single company can tackle it alone. Partnership in innovation is a much more efficient way to figure it all out, and open innovation is one such model of partnership. 100%Open, a specialist open innovation agency that has achieved a tenfold return on investment with its innovation programs,[17] gives the most appealing definition of the model: "innovating with partners by sharing risk and sharing reward." The open innovation model has been tested in a variety of industries and borne real financial fruit. In 2011, Henry Chesbrough published new research for all of us working in service industries in *Open Services Innovation: Rethinking Your Business to Grow and Compete in a New Era* (San Francisco: Jossey-Bass, 2011).

• *Stakeholder mapping* is perhaps the simplest yet most essential tool for your tool kit. It is surprising how few managers I meet are able to think in terms of stakeholder needs and risks—even within their organization, let alone outside of it. Today, stakeholder mapping is offered as a part of many project management frameworks, and it can also be practiced on its own. See "Stakeholder analysis," Wikipedia: http://en.wikipedia.org/wiki/Stakeholder_analysis.

From vertical to horizontal is the second of five essential principles that make the Overfished Ocean Strategy work—and perhaps the one that is hardest to master. The collapse of the linear throwaway economy demands a new approach to make business work: the one where you bring down the castle walls and expand your horizons beyond the competition to include the entire value chain. *Value* is the key term here: companies that make it happen discover immense value-creation opportunities they never thought possible—opportunities that can drive new and (here the term actually makes total sense!) sustainable growth. A very different kind of growth.

CHAPTER 5

Principle Three: Growth to Growth

AT A GLANCE

WE ARE USED TO growing our companies by selling more stuff to more people. But how can we keep up with that strategy in the world of increasingly stressed raw materials? It's time to make money by growing value and relevance. Stuff can wait.

"It was the best of times, it was the worst of times, it was the age of wisdom, it was the age of foolishness, it was the epoch of belief, it was the epoch of incredulity, it was the season of Light, it was the season of Darkness, it was the spring of hope, it was the winter of despair." These are the famous words with which Charles Dickens began his *Tale of Two Cities*. The world was approaching the end of the 18th century, and an entirely new idea was captivating minds and hearts all around. What if the fate of humankind was in its own hands?

"The idea that humanity could turn tables on economic necessity—mastering rather than being enslaved by material circumstances—is so new that Jane Austen never entertained it," wrote Sylvia Nasar in her extraordinary book *Grand Pursuit: The Story of Economic Genius*.

> The *typical* Englishman [of Austen's times] was a farm laborer. According to economic historian Gregory Clark, his material standard of living was not much better than that of an average Roman slave. . . . Clark estimates that the British farm laborer consumed an average of only 1500 calories a day, one-third fewer than a member of a modern hunter-gatherer tribe in New Guinea or the Amazon. . . . Yet the typical Englishman was better off than his French or German counterpart. . . . In Jane Austen's world everybody knew his or her place, and no one questioned it. A mere fifty years after her death, that world was altered beyond recognition.

Every time I reread these words, they never fail to shock me. From the days of Roman slaves to the era of my great-grandfather, the world stood still. And then, a new world was born. Jane Austen, who passed away in the summer of 1817, did not live to see this new world, where the quality of living of the absolute majority—now rigorously measured and monitored—improved beyond recognition. Nasar continued,

> The late Victorian statistician Robert Giffen found it necessary to remind his audience that in Austen's day wages had been only half as high and "periodic starvation was, in fact, the condition of the masses of working men throughout the kingdom fifty years ago . . ."

It was the sense that what had been fixed and frozen through the ages was becoming fluid. The question was no longer if conditions could change but how much, how fast, and at what cost. It was the sense that the changes were not accidental or a matter of luck, but the result of human intention, will, and knowledge.[1]

Today, we know this body of knowledge as economics.

Hard to believe? Saving the world's poor and advancing the fate of the human race is hardly what comes to mind when one thinks of economists. (That might just be my mind, though.) But the original aspirations of the science are very clear: to be, as one of the greatest economists, John Maynard Keynes, put it, "the trustees, not of civilization, but of the possibility of civilization."[2]

Somewhere, somehow, something went terribly wrong.

———

Here is what happened. In the effort to give the newborn field a solid scientific underpinning, the legendary economists of the late 19th century turned to physics to borrow some of the most modern equations of their time. The problem: the model they'd borrowed was proved wrong. Science historian Robert Nadeau explains:

> Now legendary economists—William Stanley Jevons, Léon Walras, Maria Edgeworth and Vilfredo Pareto—developed their theories by adapting equations from 19th-century physics that eventually became obsolete. . . . The physical theory that the creators of neoclassical economics used as a template was conceived in . . . 1847 [by the] German physicist Hermann von Helmholtz. [He] formulated the conservation of energy principle and postulated the existence of a field of conserved energy that fills all space and unifies these phenomena. Later in the century James Maxwell, Ludwig Boltzmann, and [others] devised better explanations for electromagnetism and thermodynamics, but in the meantime, the economists had borrowed and altered Helmholtz's equations.[3]

The approach used by the economists was simple and (let's face it!) wildly unreasonable: they simply substituted economic variables for physical ones. Energy was replaced by a measure of economic well-being titled "utility"; potential and kinetic energy was substituted by the sum of utility and expenditure. A number of renowned physicists and mathematicians made it clear to the economists that there was absolutely no reason for making these swaps, but the economists left the criticism untouched and proceeded to claim that economics had now been transformed into a truly scientific and highly vigorous discipline.

As *Scientific American* put it, "The economist has no clothes"![4]

Among the long list of assumptions made by the founders of neoclassic economics are a few crucial ones. They imagined the global market as a closed system, where natural resources, along with any potential damage to the natural environment, were set outside the boundaries of the system (the term *externality* might sound familiar). And more important: the mathematical models that have served as a foundation of modern economics assumed that there were absolutely no biological limits to economic growth. And thus the myth of never-ending, teeth-grinding, quarter-over-quarter growth was born.

But I am not here to debate the philosophy or theory of growth.

The debate on growth has been around for centuries. Indeed, the "to grow or not to grow" debate among scientists, politicians, and business leaders continues to this day. In the meantime, most of us wake up in the morning with a clear task at hand: growth! Full stop. No debate. Whether it is sales, productivity, or personal development, business today continues to measure its progress by growth—the growth of the bottom line, to be precise.

As a manager in Atlanta, Delhi, or Copenhagen, you might ask yourself, where does our growth come from? Whenever I ask this question in companies around the world, managers give me a clear and consistent answer: selling more. We are expected to sell more, day after day. Yet in a world constrained by every type of resource limitation, including landfill space, it is obvious that selling more stuff to more people as the primary growth model is rapidly becoming obsolete. Companies championing the Overfished Ocean Strategy have found another way.

By the Hour

We have all heard this tale: the economy does not stand still; it evolves over time. From agricultural to industrial to service economy and beyond, we are moving day after day. What is not being told as often, however, is that the shift from one type of economy to another is not as clear as it seems. More precisely, what we produce may stay the same. But what we sell changes dramatically.

Consider, for example, the 50-year-old story of Rolls-Royce. The name might ring a bell—after all, Rolls-Royce luxury cars are among the most recognizable brands. What the company makes most of its money on, however, is not cars—it's engines (for planes, first and foremost).

The production of airplane and other power engines is, by any means, a function of the industrial economy. It is the most bricks-and-mortar (and a lot of metal) business you can imagine. And indeed, that is what the company produces. But it is not what the company sells.

In 1962, Rolls-Royce developed an innovative solution to support the Viper engine for one of the business jets. Named Power-by-the-Hour, it offers a complete engine and accessory replacement service on a fixed-cost-per-flying-hour basis. In essence, the company took a product and turned it into a service. As a result, both manufacturer and operator got a benefit by paying only for engines that performed well, while Rolls-Royce took control of all the maintenance revenues otherwise enjoyed by local maintenance providers, along with the entire end-of-life raw material, allowing for much easier reuse of the valuable resource.

In 2002, the signature Power-by-the-Hour service became part of a much-extended service offering: Rolls-Royce CorporateCare. Among new features are Engine Health Monitoring, which tracks on-wing performance using onboard sensors; the option to lease engines to replace an operator's engine during off-wing maintenance, thereby minimizing downtime; and much more. Now, plane operators are able to manage the risk related to unscheduled maintenance events, making maintenance costs predictable. Rolls-Royce gets its engines back—turning line into circle and product into service—all while churning out the same old engines. In 2011, more than half of its annual revenues of £11.3 billion (about $17.5 billion US) came from services.[5]

Rolls-Royce's example is not the only one in the industry. The Swedish company Volvo Aero does exactly the same—selling service of well-performing aircraft turbines instead of selling the engines themselves. The customer pays per turbine spins in the air, while Volvo takes over the maintenance of the engine, providing staff with strong knowledge and skills related to the specific engine's functionality. It is a win for the customers, as the service makes it unnecessary for the flight carrier to hire specialist engineers to maintain the engines and optimized performance of the engines, leading to a reduction in fuel consumption. As a result, flight carriers save on costs for employees as well as fuel, and their engines emit less CO_2 as a result of fuel reduction. Volvo gets better revenues along with control of the engine for the entire life cycle.[6]

In the context of the collapsing linear economy, moving from products to all-around solutions becomes the easiest way to find and secure future growth. Selling safe and energy-efficient flight, rather than engines; clean surfaces, rather than chemicals; holes in the walls, rather than hammers and nails—the list goes on.

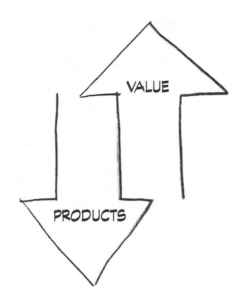

Mike Brown, former vice president of apparel giant Patagonia, spoke to *Fast Company* about the paramount importance of looking at your work as service in the context of rapid resource decline. Here is writer Charles Fishman making sense of that conversation:

> "The cutting edge, the thing that is getting more traction, is the effort to sell services rather than products," Brown says. It's a shift in perspective that can transform a business. It's IBM selling you computing services—server space, processing capacity—rather than actual computers. A company selling computers wants to sell as many servers as possible, without much regard for the power they consume or cooling they require; a company that sells computer services wants the most efficient, cool-running servers it can make. Companies that are able to turn their business inside out this way find that addressing sustainability issues can change from a burden or cost to an opportunity for efficiency and profit.[7]

The shift from products to services, Brown argues, requires a new way of looking at things, where a company would be driven to innovation and efficiency. If you are a chemical company that shifts from selling chlorine to selling disinfection, all of a sudden you are inspired to conserve chemicals, rather than push more of them to be used by the market; you have new reason to find ways to recover and recycle all raw materials. Fishman's interview with Brown clearly sparked the writer's imagination: Indeed, imagine what Nike might be like if it sold "shoe services" by subscription—the way Netflix rents movies—instead of shoes.

But selling services is just one road to a new kind of growth.

On Selling the Story

I was born in 1986, and our project has been around for barely a year. We are young, and our motto is "The young for the young!" We take underprivileged kids from the streets and teach them how to become cooks. The kids come to Ajdovscina, a small Slovene town, where we have a small restaurant, and learn aspects of economics, psychology, and cooking. We started out with seven young people from all over Slovenia, six of whom are now working. In the second class we have 12 kids. They still have two months until graduation, but two of them already have jobs.[8]

I met Matevz Slokar, founder of S Project, at a large pan-European meeting. Sandi Cesko, the president and CEO of Studio Moderna, the leading multichannel e-commerce and direct-to-consumer retail platform in Central and Eastern Europe (CEE), Russia, and Turkey, was to speak at the panel on innovation that I was moderating—and there was no question that the richest man in Slovenia was the main attraction for the hundreds of participants and journalists gathered. But after a few short remarks, Cesko asked a young man in the audience to stand up and tell his story. Suddenly, the entire auditorium woke up.

The great majority of projects similar to Slokar's are set up as nonprofits, depending on European Union grants or private donations. In contrast, S Project is set up as a private business with a solid business model. In 2012, the company had one employee but managed to earn EUR 60,000 (about $80,000 US) in revenues. By the end of 2013, the company planned to employ 30 people and make EUR 700,000 in revenues. "Everything that we earn is plowed back into the S Academy. The first initiative was about cooking, but we are developing another one that will be called S Business. It will be a business school at which we will teach young adults age 18 to 25 how to set up a project like the S Project."

So the expense side of S Project is very clear—teaching young adults—but what is the source of its revenues? What does it sell, exactly?

When the company started, it had no product. But it had something much more rare, much more difficult to find. S Project had a story. "When we set up the project, we did not have selling channels, and we did not have a product either," said Slokar. "We sent out 100 e-mails to the largest Slovene companies. The chief executive officer of a company called Steklarna Hrastnik, with 750 employees, responded that he would like to help us but he had no idea exactly how. We told him that we could sell his products using our story. This story should increase the company's profit."

Figure 4. The Speak drinking glass's story is the reason why it commands a premium price.

So the story got it all started. In collaboration with Steklarna Hrastnik designers, the S Project team designed a special kind of glass. Speak For A Higher Purpose is a rocking glass—it has a curved bottom that keeps it slightly off-balance. The glass also comes with a stabilizing base, and if turned upside down, it can be used as a candleholder.

"The vision of S Project which is looking for individuals who are apparently unreliable and unstable—however, put through S Academy, they are 'stabilized' and prepared for life on their own," says the company site. S Project's vision gave birth to the central idea for Speak glass: When you first look at it, "it is unstable and unusual. Fill it with content and it becomes reliable, unbreakable, different, and attractive. And when set on its base it is raised above the average."[9] According to Matevz Slokar, an ordinary glass of this kind would sell for around EUR 5. "With our story, it goes for EUR 20." A gigantic leap in revenues without any additional resource used. That is a new kind of growth.

With the success of Speak glass, S Project got busy designing new collaborations. S Catering was a natural next step: getting catering jobs for large corporations in search of win-win solutions for business and society. And that is exactly how Slokar met Cesko.

Studio Moderna, the company that Sandi Cesko cofounded and has run since 1992, grew out of a single product: a back-pain-relief device named Kosmodisk, sold directly over the phone. By 2007 the company had grown into a multichannel retail operation present in 21 countries with about $70 million in sales—selling many more products to many more customers. And then the world financial crisis hit. By 2013, the company had scaled up by a *factor of 10*—all the result of organic growth—and had grown to employ over 6,000 people. How exactly did they pull it off?

"The world is definitely changing, dramatically. Economy is a way that we people are using resources to fulfill our desires." Cesko speaks with remarkable precision and clarity.

This is a very simple explanation, farmer's logic. And this has shifted in the history many times: from agricultural society to industrial to information, etc., etc. We are seeing this shift happening again. And it is bigger than ever before. And what is very important is that this shift is not driven by the typical forces that worked before, it is not driven by tangible assets, by machinery, by occupation of new territory. Instead, what matters is the intangibles: speed, relationships, the way you do business. Two things happened. One is that this change is not driven by the growth of economy as we know it. Economy was growing because the demand was bigger than supply. Second is that we have faced the limits of Mother Nature. The natural resources can no longer sustain the way we want to live.[10]

Tracking these fundamental changes, Studio Moderna started a careful business-model transformation more than a decade ago. First, it moved from seeing itself as a company selling products to a company selling services. Information and education became the center of attention, and products that had the most of it brought in the biggest revenues. But that was not enough. Cesko explains:

The financial crisis has brought one change in the thinking of especially the Western population. Two years ago, the CEO of Walmart, the largest retailer in the world, said that even the purchasing power comes back to the pockets of the customer; they won't buy the same way as before. People, especially in the West, have enough stuff. Before, we were willing to buy the first car, then the second car, maybe the third car for the family; basic house, bigger house; one TV set; more and more. More is not anymore the key driving force that will make us commit. The new things are being born: it is not anymore about quantity, which is driving the world, but the quality. And the quality resides in our intangible assets. The role of the company is not to produce more and more stuff but to rethink the paradigm of how we work and how we live. In the past, we sold *products*. Today, we are selling *services*. But the global overcapacity, coupled with the resource crunch, means something new. We simply cannot possibly sell more and more stuff. Tomorrow, our capacity to sell will depend on our ability to stay relevant. We have to produce *relevance*.[11]

Building relevance into everything a company makes is not an easy task. Studio Moderna's partnership with S Project is one of many experiments aimed at making relevance happen. In April 2013, S Catering and S Academy served guests of Studio Moderna's Dinner With A Purpose, which brought up an idea for a new collaboration. The multichannel retailer produces a large number of video programs for customers eager to learn healthier cooking techniques. The cookware used in the programs is sold through Studio Moderna's channels, and now the company is partnering with S Project to produce the videos with underprivileged youths playing the central role. S Project also opened a new restaurant in Studio Moderna's headquarters, and by August 2013 it was already serving 1,000 meals each day across all locations. With quality and price of food comparable to those of existing companies, what truly differentiates S Project is the added value of helping youth with every meal purchased. More projects in product development, leadership development, marketing, and beyond are in the works. Selling stories, selling meaning, selling relevance indeed.

WHAT ARE THE STORIES that define us in light of our customers, employees, and shareholders? And are these the stories we want to tell—and have others tell about us? If the answer to these questions is no, then you must start taking the actions that will replace the old stories. Your success depends on the honesty and integrity of your actions as well as on the emotional impact they make. The cynicism created when the "stories" are proved to be false or misleading can be extremely damaging.

JOHN P. KOTTER
AUTHOR, CONSULTANT, AND HARVARD BUSINESS
SCHOOL PROFESSOR

The Power of Why

"Why is Apple so innovative?" On the small stage of TEDxPuget-Sound, Simon Sinek speaks with barely contained passion.[12] The author of *Start With Why: How Great Leaders Inspire Everyone to Take Action* (New York: Portfolio, 2009), Sinek became a darling of the TED movement, and as I watch this talk on a hot Sunday afternoon in August 2013, 11,710,415 people have already viewed it before me. His talk, too, is about selling relevance.

Apple, Sinek asserts, is just another computer company. Like everyone else on the market, they have access to the same programmers, same consultants, same advertising agencies, and same media outlets. Yet somehow, time and again, they are more innovative than their competition.

For Sinek, the secret of Apple's success is the same secret that drove the glory of Martin Luther King. While millions suffered the abuses of pre–civil rights America, it was King who led a movement that transformed the nation—and the world.

The Wright brothers, who pioneered powered human flight, also faced tough competition. Teams of professionals, many of whom were better qualified and better paid, failed to reach the goal. But somehow, it was the Wrights who managed to break through. Why is that? Sinek's theory offers one possible explanation: what unites Apple, Martin Luther King Jr., and the Wright brothers is that they all thought, acted, and communicated in the same way—and in a way that was quite distinct from everyone else. This discovery is what Sinek calls the "golden circle"—and it is the very center of his TEDx talk.

Turning his back to the audience, Sinek picks up a marker and draws three circles nestling one inside the other. In the center, he writes the word "Why." The next circle contains the word "How." "What" is placed in the last, outer circle of the three.

The *why*, the *how*, and the *what*. According to Sinek, the golden circle explains why some organizations and some leaders are able to inspire while others fall flat on their faces. The secret, he argues, is simple: most people and organizations in the world know *what* they do and are able to speak about it rather clearly. Some people and organizations know *how* they do what they do—how they are able to differentiate themselves from others and deliver a unique value or utilize a unique process. Yet very few people and organizations know *why* they do what they do—and even fewer people are able to communicate clearly what is their reason for existence, the central reason for being, the belief that propels them forward—and deserves the attention of the world.

As the answer to the question of *why* is fuzzy for most people, it is easier to hide behind the rather clear answers to the questions of *what* and *how*. As a result, most of us communicate from the outside in— moving from *what* to *how* to *why*. Sinek illustrates:

> If Apple were like everyone else, a marketing message from them might sound like this: "We make great computers [Sinek points at the "What" glowing in the outermost circle]. They're beautifully designed, simple to use, and user-friendly [Sinek's hand moves to the middle circle, pointing at the "How"]. Wanna buy one?" Meh . . . [He drops his hand, never reaching the "Why."]

And the outside-in trajectory is the way most of us speak to the world. The majority of sales, marketing, and operations—and interpersonal relations—are built around *what* and *how*, with little, if any, attention paid to the issue of *why*. Here is our new SUV (*what*). It has a powerful motor and more legroom than any other model on the market (*how*). Here is a great new restaurant (*what*). It uses local ingredients and focuses on excellent meats (*how*). It is clear and understandable—but fails to inspire. Is there an alternative?

> Here is how Apple actually communicates [Sinek's hand reaches straight for the center circle with the "Why" waiting calmly in the middle]. "Everything we do, we believe in challenging the status quo. We believe in thinking differently. [He moves on to the second circle

of "How."] The way we challenge the status quo is by making our
products beautifully designed, simple to use, and user-friendly. We
just happened to make great computers [he finishes at "What"]. Want
to buy one?" Totally different, right? All I did was reverse the order of
the information.

Sinek's passionate explanation is an invitation to consider what it
is exactly that people buy from us. To put it simply, people don't buy
what we produce—but rather fall for why we do what we do. This
approach explains why most people find it natural to buy a computer
from Apple, a phone from Apple, an MP3 player from Apple—but
we would find it harder to do so from other computer companies,
whether Dell, Gateway, or HP. In fact, most of the attempts of other
computer companies to follow Apple's suite failed miserably. Gateway,
Sinek asserts, came out with flat-screen TVs, which it has been making for years as computer monitors. Yet few got sold. Same goes for
Dell's efforts to push MP3 players and PDAs: the company has all the
capabilities and assets to produce such products, yet few customers
buy them. So why does Apple not have such a problem? For Sinek, the
answer is simple: people fall not for what you do but for why you do it.

Simon Sinek's theory of "why" is one way to look at the success
of companies like S Project and Studio Moderna—companies that
bet their future growth on selling the stories, selling relevance. In the
world of limited resources, stuff is overrated. What matters is the ability to look at what you do. What matters is meaning—and the good
news is that meaning comes in unlimited forms, with unlimited supply. It does, however, require significant skill and a carefully selected
set of tools.

Building Your Tool Kit

Transition from one type of growth to another definitely involves a
change of mind-set. A number of different theories, techniques, and
approaches have been developed. They might look like a diverse if

not an odd bunch, but it is all about trial and error: what works for your company and your industry might be completely irrelevant for another. Here are a few *growth-to-growth* tools you might consider for your own Overfished Ocean Strategy tool kit:

- I have referred to Trendwatching.com in nearly every chapter so far, as I really do like their unorthodox take on consumer trends. The company tracks a number of patterns in consumer behavior, along with different subpatterns and forces, and all the interconnections between them. The top-level report, which is usually produced once a year as a forecast for the year to come, gives you a big-picture view of what is going on. But dig into each trend and you will find plenty of data, sense making, and examples of business innovation turning the trend into a successful business model. "Localizasian," "Pretail," "Newism," "Flawsome"—these are just a few of the trends on the recent list. You can find more at http://www.trendwatching.com/.

- Moving from product to service is a process that has been tried and tested for a long time. You can find new ideas from a movement that has become known as *servitization*. A simple Web search will offer you a range of conferences, videos, and articles on how it works. But to start you with clear routes in the right direction, the work of Soren Kaplan might come in handy. See his January 18, 2013, article, "How to Think About Turning Your Products Into Services," on the *Fast Company* website.[13]

- While turning products into services is key, going beyond toward relevance and transformation is yet another step up. Among many changes professed to follow eras of the knowledge and service economies, the "experience economy" offers the most innovative takes on the same old routine. The idea of the experience economy is far from new, and a 1998 *Harvard Business Review* article solidified the approach as the next best thing. The authors used a birthday cake to demonstrate the entire economic progression from agricultural to industrial to service to experience. Baking a birthday cake at home using typical farm commodities, such as eggs, flour, and milk, was replaced by the industrial solution: a baking mixture was prepared for you and sold in a convenient, colorful box. The service economy took over—the entire baking service was provided by the store or a bakery shop—only to give way to professionally orchestrated birthday solutions—remarkable experiences (birthday cake included). What is noticeable is that each transition represents a giant leap in value. The authors explain: "Economists have typically lumped experiences in with services, but experiences are a distinct economic offering, as different from services as services are from goods. Today we can identify and describe this fourth economic offering because consumers unquestionably desire experiences, and more and more businesses are responding by explicitly designing and promoting them."[14] Experiments with the experience economy might offer you and your company ideas for discovering new opportunities for growth, without any new strain on your supply chain and a subsequent increase in costs. You might start your exploration with the article itself.

———————

Until now, we have been focusing on Overfished Ocean Strategy principles that focus on the factors and forces outside of the company walls—growth being one of them. But to be successful "out there," we must also get everything in order "in here," helping the company itself to start working in a new way. The last two principles aim at exactly that: figuring out how the company should organize itself. Planning will be our first stop.

CHAPTER 6

Principle Four: Plan to Model

AT A GLANCE

MODERN MANAGEMENT HAS A thing for putting life in boxes. We are obsessed with making neat, controllable plans broken into clear, manageable steps. Yet the companies mastering the Overfished Ocean Strategy seem to live in a different universe—one that is messy, iterative, and full of happy (and devastating) accidents. Every company that dared to venture into the unknown terrain *from line to circle* had to do so in the near dark, each step leading to the next, experimenting, taking action, and producing results long before a truly comprehensive strategy could be articulated. In other words, they had to learn their way into the Overfished Ocean Strategy. Welcome to the exciting world of continuous business modeling.

It happens to me with a surprising frequency. A short e-mail, a quick phone call, a Facebook post, and suddenly you feel like all is right with the world. Like there is true justice. Like good guys really do finish first.

This was one of those e-mails.

Brief and to the point, professional as ever, Iztok Seljak, president of the Management Board of Hidria, shared the happy news: beating more than 15,000 other companies, Hidria Corporation won the title of Europe's most innovative company of 2013. That put a smile on my face!

Over the past decade, Seljak, a fearless leader, an inspiring colleague, and a frequent speaker at my executive MBA classes, has championed his team to invent its way out of disappearance. A company with a rich past, Hidria found itself in search of new history by the early 2000s.[1] With its core competence in producing electric motors for cooling and heating systems, the question was: Is there anywhere else this skill might be useful? It turned out there was.

With the turn of the century, the pressure to reduce harmful emissions, coupled with rapid growth in the price of fuel and the development of battery technology and infrastructure, finally made an electric motor into a legitimate new business idea. Figure 5 shows one way to visualize this pressure.[2]

The left side of the graph represents the amount of emissions that European Union regulation allowed for passenger cars under the EU I mandate. The right side of the graph represents the amount of emissions permitted under the EU VI mandate, including minuscule permissible levels of particulate matter (PM) hiding in the bottom-right corner. It is easy to notice that all permissible levels have gone down at a staggering rate, with the burden of innovation to meet the legal demands pressing heavy on the backs of car manufacturers. While fuel cell and other technologies are still far from mass commercialization, the introduction of electric motors for hybrid or pure electric vehicles was the easiest way to meet the demands of the new legislation. The

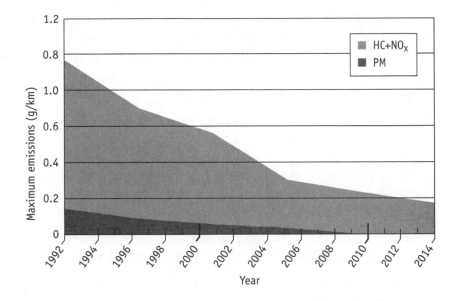

Figure 5. Emissions of hydrocarbon, nitrogen oxide, and particulates allowable for diesel passenger cars under EU regulations between 1992 and 2014.

problem was that very few automotive powerhouses in the world had a strong competence in building an electric motor, and even fewer automotive suppliers had been innovating in this domain.

But a company producing electric motors for air conditioning and heating systems did. In 2004, Hidria turned its business on its head by adding "green" mobility to its mission, vision, and core strategy. In the first year of operations, 2005, the new automotive division brought in EUR 10 million (about $13 million US) in revenues. By 2012, amid the global economic recession, Hidria reached the profitable automotive revenues of EUR 150 million (nearly $200 million US). Today, the engine of every fifth new diesel-powered car globally is ignited by Hidria's ignition solutions, every fifth new car in Europe is steered by Hidria's electrical power-steering solutions, and every third new car in Europe is powered by Hidria's hybrid and electrical power-train solutions, including esteemed top-of-the-line models produced by Audi, BMW, Mercedes-Benz, Porsche, Ford, Peugeot, Renault, and Volkswagen. It took a mere seven years. That's all.

There is no question that everyone likes this kind of Cinderella story: from nothing to top of the world in a few easy steps. The most interesting question, of course, is: How did Hidria get there?

————

"Why did we enter electric mobility? We were young, full of new ideas, and hungry to go beyond following to leading. When we started, the entire automotive industry had already proclaimed this domain of innovation as a worthless, short-lived fad nondeserving of any significant attention. Thankfully, we did not know that at the time." The entire Executive MBA classes chuckles as Seljak reflects back. But that is exactly where the secret of Hidria's success lies: the ability to constantly look at their business anew. They call it "embedded business model innovation."

Seljak explains: "They all think that it is all about technological innovation. That, of course, is important. But it is not what truly makes the difference. Time and again, our victories depend on the ability to imagine an entirely new way of adding value. That is what business model innovation is about—value creation, reimagined. Continuously."

Hidria's success has been built on this approach. When the company developed new technology suitable for a hybrid motorbike, the OEM decided to neglect the innovation as hardly appealing to the traditional rough-around-the-edges, testosterone-driven biker bunch. Refusing to take no for an answer, Hidria, which had no knowledge of business-to-consumer communications, developed a comprehensive marketing and communications package built around the idea of "One bike, two hearts" to combat the negative image of hybrid technology among lovers of motorsport. This ability to go beyond technology transformed a newcomer into a development supplier—and then into a predevelopment supplier, serving as a true thinking partner to car companies well before a particular model is developed.

But the embedded business-model innovation is not contained within a particular product line or division. All divisions of Hidria got on board with thinking differently—and imagining an entirely new set of solutions for a resource-deprived world. With three new research-and-development institutes (each stocked with a range of laboratories), the company is constantly pushing forward with development of comprehensive, financially viable mobility and indoor air services. Turning solar power into a cooling/air-conditioning system (instead of a heating and electricity system) is a technical innovation; figuring out how to make it work financially as a viable product is a business-model innovation. Often, Hidria alone cannot achieve such innovation, so the company uses a number of "coopetition" projects, collaborating with its competitors for whole-system (remember, horizontal, not vertical!) breakthroughs. In 2011, together with seven of its competitors and the Slovenian government, Hidria became a founding partner of a new for-profit private public partnership, SiEVA, focused on codevelopment of technological solutions for ecologically clean cars.[3] In 2012, the company initiated a new sustainable-construction consortium, putting its climate-control solutions to good use. Uniting more than 40 companies across Europe, the Feniks consortium today brings together a workforce of 35,000 people with an annual revenue of EUR 4.5 billion (around $6 billion US). Building for the Sochi 2014 Olympics is among the first big victories for the consortium.

Now an award-winning initiative, Feniks justifies its existence in this way:

> We live in the era of significant global changes, requiring an ever-increased sustainability of our overall future development. Along with the ongoing economic crisis, we are facing new challenges and numerous new opportunities also for sustainable construction. Today, we burn 40 percent of fossil fuels through buildings—i.e., to cover their demands. Sustainable construction, due to its overall importance, is

becoming one of the most important segments in the focus of development of the European Union and wider. Concrete goals have been set, including a decrease in energy consumption, increase of available energy from renewable sources, minimization of harmful effects on the environment, and profound care for natural resources, while following the key guidelines of creativity and innovation.

In the coming years, construction is therefore set to go through considerable shifts and changes in overall concept, design, and execution. As a result, organizations that will be able to integrate and efficiently manage all of the required key building blocks for providing the sustainable buildings of the future will be gaining in importance. The new approaches in construction will include the ability to integrate the buildings in the natural environment in ways not known so far, and the ability to finance and/or manage the buildings' vital functions longer term, providing the lowest life-cycle costs and offering the maximum of indoor well-being. As a consequence, the role of cooperation and partnerships, gathering the best global knowledge, will also be gaining in importance. In order to proactively, comprehensively address all of these core issues, we are gathering the most creative and innovative construction companies in southeastern Europe, with rich tradition and new creative ideas and required competences to realize them. Traditional presence and important references in and around the Russian Federation, the Near and Middle East, and Northern Africa, as well as new, innovative breakthrough solutions in proprietary digitalized tools for virtual construction, complete energy management systems, innovative systems of thermo-solar and photovoltaic solutions, and new materials and processes, are all ensuring the best integration of excellent individual niche competences of each of the Feniks members into an exclusive flexible and highly competitive set of turnkey capabilities for sustainable buildings of the future.[4]

That is what inventing a new business model looks like. United we stand!

Around the world, companies similar to Hidria are waking up to the disappearing linear throwaway economy—and discovering ways to embed a new thinking into their strategy, products, and operations. Their approach is anything but "normal." In fact, normal—statistically speaking—looks entirely different.

Your New Modeling Career

What do we do when we want to launch something new? How do we turn a hunch, an idea, into a true, commercially successful innovation?

The "normal" decades-old path looks something like this: develop a solid, detailed plan (five years seems to be the assumption behind most business plans); get financial backing (budget approval in the existing corporation or investment/loan for a start-up); develop your product to perfection; and sell as much as you can.

The reality of the overfished ocean, however, throws a serious curveball into this well-known trajectory. In the face of the collapsing linear throwaway economy, resources and expectations are becoming increasingly volatile. Oil prices alone can bring the entire economy into shock. McKinsey estimates that a price of $125 to $150 a barrel, sustained for years, "would drive down global growth by 0.6 to 0.9 percentage points in the first year. Over time, as economies adjusted to the new higher prices (and shifted to different types of fuel, technologies, and production techniques), the impact would diminish. But the rate of global GDP growth would be affected for years. By 2020, the global economy would be between $1.1 trillion and $1.7 trillion smaller than the baseline outlook: the equivalent of losing Spain's or Italy's output for a year."[5] The price volatility of every other commodity is no walk in the park, either—plus, consumer, investor, and legislative pressures are equally unpredictable, intensified by radical transparency and easier-than-ever consumer and civil activism, all fueled by the advancements in social media technology.

In the world of overfished oceans, planning is overrated. In the face of extreme uncertainty, plans become obsolete in no time. The only way to make the new reality work is to find a way to constantly adapt your business to the new reality—treating it as a strategic priority rather than a short-lived sidekick to the core business. And for the companies mastering the Overfished Ocean Strategy, business modeling, rather than strategic planning, is the name of the game. Unlike cumbersome, static, and rigid plans, models are agile, evolving, and open to change. Modeling, rather than planning, is the key to turning *line into circle*—and making money in the process.

In contrast to business strategy, which is essentially about the best *way* to get from point A to point B, a business model is about the *vehicle* you use for traveling—the mechanism that allows you to create, deliver, and capture value. An essential element of strategy development, a business model is a design—a unique combination of driving forces that allow you to enact a commercial opportunity.

In 2010, a group of 470 practitioners led by Alexander Osterwalder and Yves Pigneur cocreated a common language for what a business model looks like when developed and communicated within and beyond the company.[6] Known as a Business Model Canvas, the tool helps us grasp value creation in a clear and simple picture that looks something like Figure 6.

A simple and clean tool, the canvas helps us capture the essence of our business model—and figure out a new way to reinvent it. The process is so simple that it is almost ridiculous. To start, you take a product or a service and fill out the canvas with every bit of detail. You might be surprised to discover completely different ways to understand your customers and their needs—and then create real value delivered in the most meaningful way. Continuous business-model innovation is the systematic reimagining of the key driving forces within the model—and rethinking the way each driving force relates to the others.

Consider, for example, the story of OneWorld Health, founded in 2000 as the first nonprofit pharmaceutical company in the United

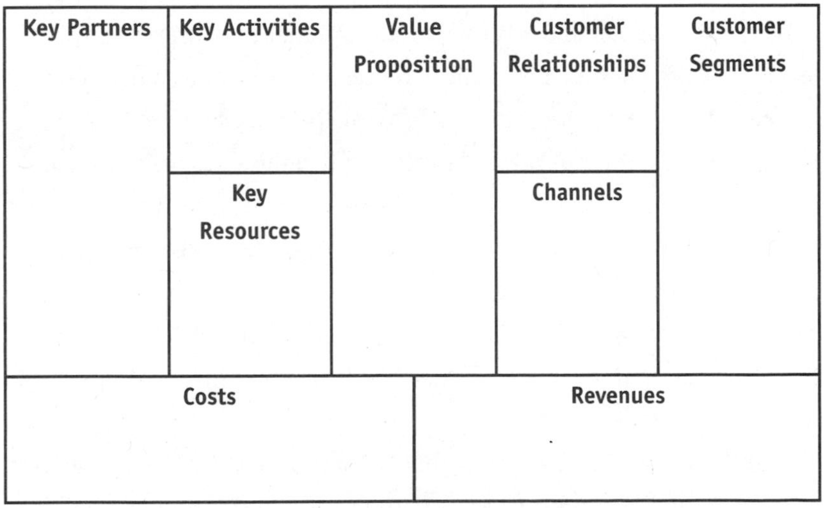

Key Partners	Key Activities	Value Proposition	Customer Relationships	Customer Segments
	Key Resources		Channels	
Costs			Revenues	

Figure 6. The Business Model Canvas offers a great exercise for understanding and strengthening your value creation.

States. When Drs. Victoria Hale and Ahvie Herskowitz decided to start the company, the problem was simple: hundreds of millions of people around the world were suffering from what became known as *orphan diseases*—Third World malaises that no Western pharmaceutical company wanted to take on for the lack of a substantial profit prospect. The solution: develop a business model that would turn orphan diseases into a viable opportunity. Since much of the pharmaceutical investment goes into the research-and-development pipeline—searching for drug leads and then developing them via an expensive trial process—OneWorld Health realized early that they needed to find another process to fit their pocketbook. The company leaders also realized that many pharmaceutical businesses already had drug leads for orphan diseases—which they had discovered accidentally while researching other drugs—that were sitting idle on the shelves as wasted resources. OneWorld Health went to for-profit pharmaceutical companies and suggested that they donate drug leads that had little commercialization potential in the West, with the benefit of a tax deduction. Then the company worked on developing the leads into safe and effective medicines in partnership with scientists and manufacturers in the developing world, thus significantly reducing the costs and bringing the medicine to consumers at an affordable price.

The success of OneWorld Health had little to do with *technical* innovation, as the company uses rather mainstream technologies that are well developed and far from new to make things happen. Instead, this pharmaceutical company thrived due to *business-model* innovation—connecting different stakeholders in a unique and inventive way to deliver new value. Business modeling is fast becoming the competence to master.

The American company Safechem, a subsidiary of Dow Chemical, changed its business model from selling products to selling services— providing customers with a complete cleaning service instead of selling chemical cleaning products. The service is based on a closed-loop *line-to-circle* system where solvents are delivered, used, and taken back. Customers are billed on the basis of product performance—for example, chemicals used per square foot instead of per product used. That way, Safechem's revenue depends on the volume of cleaned surface instead of the volume of solvents sold, making its business model much more resource intelligent. It is estimated that Safechem's chemical leasing service has the potential to reduce solvent usage by 63 percent—and mitigate many other environmental impacts.[7] Again, the company's performance—including cost savings on chemicals—was the result of business-model reinvention rather than any kind of technological breakthrough.

Norwegian company Allfarveg is an example of a business-model innovation based on the design-build-finance-operate (DBFO) model. DBFO business undertakes capital-intensive, long-term construction projects where private finance, construction, service, and/or maintenance are bundled into a long-term, multidecade contract. Such contracts provide the incentive to improve the quality of the construction, thus lowering the life-cycle costs of the projects. Allfarveg was created to design, build, finance, operate, and maintain the new road between Lyngdal and Flekkefjord in Norway. Having a 25-year contract with the Norwegian Public Roads Administration, Allfarveg gets paid based on the performance of the road. Such an incentive structure led Allfarveg to implement a number of not-so-usual techniques and solutions, such as using brighter stones in the asphalt, which require less light intensity to illuminate the road at night. This simple change resulted in a 30 percent reduction in electricity costs and a savings in resources used for electricity—all while the road-construction work was completed two years ahead of time.[8] That is business-model innovation.

THE SAME PRODUCTS, SERVICES, or technologies can fail or succeed depending on the business model you choose. Exploring the possibilities is critical to finding a successful business model. Settling on first ideas risks the possibility of missing potential that can only be discovered by prototyping and testing different alternatives.

ALEXANDER OSTERWALDER
AUTHOR, *BUSINESS MODEL GENERATION*

Companies and managers mastering Overfished Ocean Strategy do something different. They take the collapse of the linear throwaway economy as an opportunity to rethink their entire strategy and use it as a source of business-model innovation. They abandon the heavy, static, flawed plans and develop the capacity for deliberate and continuous business-model innovation, increasing their own agility and adaptability in the process. And it happens to be one of the leanest, most efficient ways of running your organization.

Leaning Up

In spring 2013, my husband and I decided to enter into a new business. As the negotiations with the potential partners started in March, among the first key documents for us to explore—and work on— was a business plan. Intense work by a whole team of solid thinkers produced a document of solid assumptions, clear goals, and extensive coordinated steps to achieve them. Since we took on the task of upgrading an existing business with an existing product, by the end of April, we were rolling. By late May, the prices of raw materials and transportation shifted while sales results suggested an entirely new opportunity. Our business plan became obsolete.

It turns out we were not alone. Increasingly, companies big and small, new and existing, are figuring out that the traditional model of planning, product development, and execution generates wasted resources and marginal returns—resources that our resource-deprived economy can no longer afford. A new movement has emerged that makes this process less wasteful and less risky. And it borrows its key principles from a concept central to resource intelligence: lean manufacturing.

In 1937, a small company manufacturing automatic looms for the textile industry produced an unusual spinoff—a newborn daughter business focused on the needs of the automotive industry. By July 2012, this little child had grown to become the 11th-largest company in the world by revenue and produced its 200 millionth vehicle. It had also created one of the best-known operations and manufacturing philosophies in the world—the Toyota Production System.

Built on the idea that nothing should go to waste, and every resource used in business should directly contribute to value, Toyota's approach was expanded and enhanced to become *lean manufacturing*[9]—the term coined by John Krafcik in his 1988 article "Triumph of the Lean Production System," published in the *Sloan Management Review*.[10] The idea of *lean* is simple: everything we do should be useful; nothing we do should be wasteful. A simple waste of time—such as employees' waiting for supplies to be delivered to the manufacturing line from the central warehouse—decreases our productivity, but that is not the only waste. When we sit and wait, we are also using the real estate inefficiently: we waste energy, water, and other raw materials used to run an idle plant, and all of that is multiplied by waste generated at every other step of production, sucked into our bottleneck. An alternative? Develop a lean mind-set—a way of looking at your business from a waste-less prospective.

Traditionally, the idea of lean has been focused on the operations process itself, rather than business strategy. But the movement born in the past few years took the concept of lean to an entirely new level—applying it to starting up new businesses, new divisions and products, new strategies. Welcome to the *lean start-up*.

Here is how new things get started in business (most of the time). First, the company starts with a product or service idea, which immediately gets backed by a business plan. After a few months, in the most painful way, the entrepreneurs discover that the plan has failed. In a 2013 *Harvard Business Review* article, Steve Blank explained the reasons:

> Business plans rarely survive the first contact with customers. As the boxer Mike Tyson once said about his opponents' prefight strategies, "Everybody has a plan until they get punched in the mouth." No one besides venture capitalists and the late Soviet Union requires five-year plans to forecast complete unknowns. These plans are generally fiction, and dreaming them up is almost always a waste of time. . . . The founders of lean start-ups don't begin with a business plan; they begin with the search for a business model. Only after quick rounds of experimentation and feedback reveal a model that works do lean founders focus on execution.[11]

The lean start-up model, while developed for new enterprises, offers a wonderful framework for companies interested in conquering the overfished ocean. While the traditional business focuses on business plans, lean start-ups concentrate on business models. While the majority build their products after full specification and launch them with the help of a linear, step-by-step plan, lean enterprises get out of the office and test their hypotheses, building their products iteratively and incrementally with a lot of customer input. And while most of us treat failure as a rare, unexpected abnormality, lean companies expect failures as the right and necessary element of business-model innovation—and fix them by iterating the ideas away from the features that did not work.

The model championed by the lean start-up movement is exactly
what the Overfished Ocean Strategy companies have been doing for
years, if not decades. The secret of making this strategy work is to
move from business *plan* to business *model*—and experiment relentlessly with products, services, and processes for continuous radical
innovation. As you develop your *plan-to-model* skills, a few tools
might come handy.

FAMOUS PIVOT STORIES ARE often failures, but you don't
need to fail before you pivot. All a pivot is is a change
[in] strategy without a change in vision. Whenever
entrepreneurs see a new way to achieve their vision—a
way to be more successful—they have to remain nimble
enough to take it.

ERIC RIES
AUTHOR, *THE LEAN STARTUP: HOW TODAY'S
ENTREPRENEURS USE CONTINUOUS INNOVATION TO
CREATE RADICALLY SUCCESSFUL BUSINESSES*

Building Your Tool Kit

Starting with the first homework in kindergarten, we are trained to
conquer our world with a solid plan. As we grow, the plans get bigger, becoming their own art form once the level of business planning
is reached. But in the world of disappearing resources, collapsing
landfills, and increasing expectations from customers and every other
stakeholder, planning is a futile activity doomed from the get-go.
Business modeling, in contrast, offers a solid pathway to creating,
delivering, and capturing value that is much more nimble, real-time,
and appropriate for the reality of the overfished ocean. A good set of
tools has been developed and polished by hundreds of business prac-

titioners—and might just offer the perfect *plan-to-model* pathway. Here are a few you might consider for your own Overfished Ocean Strategy tool kit:

- The community behind the Business Model Canvas has been growing by the minute, with countless resources available online. The IDEO innovation and design agency offers great tools for business-model visualization; you can find their videos on YouTube, as well as resources and cases from their Business Design division on their website at http://www.ideo.com /expertise/business-design/.

  A 2010 book that made this movement explode is titled *Business Model Generation: A Handbook for Visionaries, Game Changers, and Challengers*, by Alexander Osterwalder and Yves Pigneur, developers of the Business Model Canvas described earlier in the chapter, and it has a very strong, vibrant presence, online and via face-to-face gatherings. Here, you can find a free 70-page preview of the book, a list of events you can join in your country, tools, videos, and much more. There is also an app that allows you to create your own business-model canvases in a blink of the eye, as well as an app called Strategizer that allows you to collaborate with your team, perform all essential calculations, learn essentials through minicourses, and manage the entire project with clear tools. Learn more about business-model generation at http://www .businessmodelgeneration.com/.

- The *lean start-up movement* is another excellent resource for the rationale and practice of the transition *from plan to model*. The poster child for the movement is the 2011 book by Eric Ries titled *The Lean Startup: How Today's Entrepreneurs Use Continuous Innovation to Create Radically Successful Businesses* (New York: Crown Business), and you can learn more about the movement, including a few great cases, at http://theleanstartup.com/.

Many other articles, books, and tools have been developed based on this idea. Tim O'Reilly, CEO of O'Reilly Media, described the benefit of this approach in the following way: "The Lean Startup isn't just about how to create a more successful entrepreneurial business . . . it's about what we can learn from those businesses to improve virtually everything we do. I imagine Lean Startup principles applied to government programs, to healthcare, and to solving the world's great problems. It's ultimately an answer to the question 'How can we learn more quickly what works, and discard what doesn't?'"[12] If this level of efficiency and resourcefulness sounds right for you, you might start exploring the lean-start-up model with Steve Blank's article "Why the Lean Start-Up Changes Everything," which appeared in the May 2013 issue of *Harvard Business Review*: http://hbr.org/2013/05/why-the-lean-start-up -changes-everything.

- While both of these movements have been around for just a few years, the idea of holistic, adaptive, emergent strategic thinking is by no means new. Henry Mintzberg, one of the best strategy and learning thinkers of our time, made the case for a more emergent approach to strategy in his 1994 book appropriately titled *The Rise and Fall of Strategic Planning* (Englewood Cliffs, NJ: Prentice Hall). He spoke of the rise of strategic planning, which in the mid-1960s was hailed as "the one best way" to develop and implement strategies for achieving a competitive advantage for every business unit. It was then, following the suit of scientific management pioneered by Frederick Taylor, that companies decided to separate thinking from doing, giving birth to a new corporate function—strategic planning. Fifty years after that fateful decision, and 20 years after his book on planning came out, Mintzberg's words are as powerful as ever: "Planning systems were expected to produce the best strategies as well as step-by-step instructions for carrying out those strategies so that the doers, the managers of business, could not get them wrong. As we now know, planning has not exactly worked out that way. While certainly not dead, business planning has fallen from its pedestal. But even now, few people fully understand the reason: strategic planning is not strategic thinking. Indeed, strategic planning often spoils strategic thinking, causing managers to confuse real vision with manipulation of numbers. And this confusion lies at the heart of the issue: the most successful strategies are visions, not plans."

Business modeling is the process of describing and organizing the vision in a compelling and clear way, thus making you able to inspire and mobilize everyone involved. In your transition *from plan to model*, Henry Mintzberg's work might be very helpful. You can start by exploring his January–February 1994 *Harvard Business Review* article, whose title humorously turned the name of his book upside down: "The Fall and Rise of Strategic Planning"; http://staff.neu.edu.tr/~msagsan/files/fall-rise-of-strategic-planning_72538.pdf.

––––––––––

Transitioning from planning to modeling—like any other principle of the Overfished Ocean Strategy—is one solid way to power up innovation for a resource-deprived world. Yet to make this strategy work, one more crucial transition must take place. Often, this one is the most difficult of all.

CHAPTER 7

Principle Five:
Department to Mind-Set

AT A GLANCE

DIVISION OF LABOR HAS been around for millennia. From the ancient Sumerians to Plato to Henry Ford, everyone seems to champion the divide-and-conquer approach. Yet when a complete overhaul of strategic thinking is required, putting the transformation on the shoulders of a few is simply not good enough. The Overfished Ocean Strategy is not a department. It's a mind-set.

"Well then, how will our state supply these needs? It will need a farmer, a builder, and a weaver, and also, I think, a shoemaker and one or two others to provide for our bodily needs. . . . So that the minimum state would consist of four or five men."[1] With these words, written around 380 BC, Plato solidified the division of labor as the cornerstone of our lives—and the central functional principle of any organization as large as a state or as small as a family.

This was not a new invention. The ancient Sumerians, who had preceded Plato by a few millennia, developed and implemented the concept of the division of labor with clear jobs assigned to inhabitants of ancient cities. By the time the word *department* was first used in 1735,[2] the modern corporation had begun its slow conquest of the world, growing in size, complexity, and compartmentalization. Dividing the work in the form of clearly marked departments seemed like a perfect idea—so perfect, in fact, that by 1922 the bureaucracy model was hailed as the ideal form of organization. It was Max Weber, one of the greatest sociologists of all time and a specialist on the topic, who elevated the status of the concept:

> From a purely technical point of view, a bureaucracy is capable of attaining the highest degree of efficiency, and is in this sense formally the most rational known means of exercising authority over human beings. It is superior to any other form in precision, in stability, in the stringency of its discipline, and in its reliability. It thus makes possible a particularly high degree of calculability of results for the heads of the organization and for those acting in relation to it. It is finally superior both in intensive efficiency and in the scope of its operations and is formally capable of application to all kinds of administrative tasks.[3]

The highest degree of efficiency, the ability to predict and control results, reliability—no wonder managers of the 20th century took the idea of bureaucracy as perfect and started structuring their companies as perfectly humanless machines. Until the 1990s, it all went well. Then, the magic started to give out a little. Well, a lot.

The collapse of the Soviet Union and Yugoslavia signaled the beginning of a new era of globalization. Then came the Internet, the dot-com crisis, 9/11, the rise of China, the social media revolution, Generation Y, the global economic crisis of 2008—all against the backdrop of rapidly declining resources and the collapse of our linear throwaway economy. As a reflection of the rapid speed of change, a whole new area of business thought was developed—named, appropriately, *change management*. We did not have much change to manage before the 1990s. Now we do, and the idea of a perfectly controlled bureaucracy made up of neatly stacked departments can hardly coexist with the reality of the rapidly changing world. But somehow, we still live with it.

"This is the job description of a hospital janitor," begins Barry Schwartz in his February 2009 TED talk titled "Our Loss of Wisdom." The list presented on a large screen appears to be perfectly unremarkable. Among the items in the job description are all the things you would expect: mopping and sweeping the floors, emptying the trash, restocking the cabinets. Yet one thing the speaker wants you to become aware of: while the items are many, not one of them involves another human being. The janitor's job at a hospital could easily be done at a mortuary. No difference at all.

Schwartz has been studying the link between psychology and economics (and writing about it for the *New York Times*) for ages. Now, *wisdom* is the object of his inquiry. Wisdom among hospital janitors is a striking example.

Consider, for example, the stories of Mike, Charlene, and Luke, all shared in this talk. When psychologists interviewed Mike, they discovered that he had stopped mopping the floors when the patient was out of his bed, walking slowly up and down the hall to build up his strength. Charlene shared that she ignored her supervisor's demands and did not vacuum the visitors' lounge, as the family visitors, who spent day after day in the hospital, happened to be taking a short nap. There was also Luke, who told the researchers of washing a floor twice in the room of a young man in a coma. His father, who nearly lived in that room for six months, did not see Luke do it the first time and got angry. It is precisely these little acts of kindness, rather than any items in the job description of the janitor, that bring about huge improvements in patient care and make hospitals better. For Schwartz, these actions are a sign of something much more.

> A wise person knows when and how to make the exception to every rule, as the janitors knew when to ignore the job duties in the service of other objectives. A wise person knows how to improvise, as Luke did when he rewashed the floor. Real-world problems are often ambiguous and ill defined, and the context is always changing. A wise person is like a jazz musician—using the notes on the page but dancing around them, inventing combinations that are appropriate for the situation and the people at hand. . . . And finally, perhaps most important, a wise person is made, not born. The good news is, you don't need to be brilliant to be wise. The bad news is that without wisdom, brilliance isn't enough. It's as likely to get you and other people into trouble as anything else.[4]

Resource intelligence is not an easy-to-follow principle. *Line-to-circle* thinking cannot depend on narrow functional brilliance. The Overfished Ocean Strategy does not fit into a small box or a department. It requires a whole new mind-set—exactly what Barry Schwartz calls "practical wisdom"—a particular way of looking at the world. And acting on it.

IF I HAD AN hour to solve a problem and my life depended on the solution, I would spend the first 55 minutes determining the proper question to ask, for once I know the proper question, I could solve the problem in less than five minutes.

ALBERT EINSTEIN
PHYSICIST

In Search of a Scapegoat

The majority of companies I met got it wrong.

Most of them remain oblivious to the reality of the disappearing linear economy, unable to grasp disparate information and make sense of it in a comprehensive and systemic way. Imagine, for example, that you are a producer of jeans, a product most of us have enjoyed. Who should be responsible for tracking and managing the risks associated with volatile raw materials?

Procurers come to mind first—they are the ones bringing the raw materials in, right? But we all know that procurement simply follows the product specifications and volume requirements, having no power to change anything once the product is developed. Should it be marketing—the sensor of the market? Most companies are focused predominantly on the end consumer of the product or service, trying to either figure out a clear need or develop something we did not know we couldn't live without. R&D, then? They are the researchers before the developers, so shouldn't they know the trends related to the prices of cotton, chemicals for jeans washing, metal, or transportation? Yes, but in the case of this product, just like many others, they are designers first, bending the world to their creative vision and not the other way around. I will skip accounting and finance, the first being primarily concerned with the past and the second being obsessed with financing the business model as it is (rather than developing a new one). Who is it, then—a strategist? That seems like a perfect choice—this is, after all, survival, which is an issue of highest strategic importance. So let's make this poor fella the scapegoat. The problem is that after decades of traditional growth strategy approaches (based on *a linear view of the economy, vertical thinking*, and *traditional planning*), there are hardly any strategy professionals capable of fighting this battle as lone rangers.

As a result, obscure but essential raw material might disappear before anyone notices and prepares an alternative. Volatile weather might drive a significant segment of your customer base to any geographical location. Water might become unavailable—or beyond expensive—in a matter of months. The list goes on and on.

THE SEARCH FOR A scapegoat is the easiest of all hunting expeditions.

PRESIDENT DWIGHT D. EISENHOWER

But that is not the worst thing that could happen. There are also a growing number of companies that (with the best intentions) responded to the issue of the collapsing linear economy by creating a sustainability department, some even boasting a position of vice president of sustainability. New people are hired (on this sunny August 2012 day, CareerBuilder.com had 1,295 positions) or transferred into the department (usually from PR; HR; or environmental, health, and safety departments), a budget is defined, the chain of command is established. In the majority of cases, such departments have little power and authority within the company. And herein lies trouble.

Whenever I ask executives to imagine an invitation to a company meeting on sustainability, they consistently name it among the most dreaded kinds of meetings to avoid at all costs. They do that for a range of issues we will discuss in the "green is dead" tête-à-tête in chapter 8. But even more so, the avoidance of all corporate sustainability efforts is a natural by-product of the obsessive compartmentalization our businesses seem to suffer from. Dividing our companies into neatly stacked departments—coupled with the speed and intensity of our everyday life—leads to a constant blame game. Marketing blaming production for not fulfilling the orders, production killing marketing for promising what cannot be achieved . . . Sound familiar? The same scapegoating happens when it comes to a *line-to-circle* transition, but to a much greater degree. While the overfished oceans remain invisible to most, any work in the area is looked down on as a dreaded fad or time-wasting PR stunt. Most managers find it distracting, irrelevant, and wasteful—an annoying addition to the already overburdened to-do list. "I am busting my butt as it is, have to deal with those idiots in sales, and you are asking me to waste my time on what? Give me a break!"

It is time to move *from department to mind-set.*

The New Competencies of Knauf Insulation

"Knauf Insulation is pleased to announce that from August 2013, all four of its UK manufacturing plants will be sending zero waste to landfill."[5] With over EUR 1.2 billion (about $1.6 billion US) in 2012 revenues and more than 5,000 employees, Knauf Insulation has many reasons to celebrate. After years of work on rethinking its entire strategy and operations, the company has begun to show breakthrough results in navigating the murky waters of the overfished oceans toward a real and inimitable competitive advantage.

Knauf Insulation's business logic is simple. The slow disintegration of the linear economy offers a number of opportunities across the entire value chain. Why not use it to drive the development of new products, new processes, and new revenue streams for years to come?

On the product side, in recent years, due to pressure from volatile energy prices, the idea of zero-energy zero-carbon buildings (built environments with zero net energy consumption and zero carbon emissions annually) has gained significant traction among legislators and the public. According to Navigant (formerly known as Pike) Research, global revenue from the zero-carbon building market should hit $690 billion by 2020 and will nearly double by 2035.[6] With a compound annual growth rate of 43 percent, no wonder Knauf Insulation took the zero-energy buildings as its flagship product development effort—launching such products as mineral wool with ECOSE Technology.[7] The new wool is manufactured from natural and recycled raw materials and is bonded using a bio-based technology free from formaldehyde, phenols, and acrylics—replacing costly artificially synthesized petroleum-based chemicals. It has a natural brown color; no artificial colors, bleaches, or dyes are used in the processing. For installers, the new wool is softer and easier to handle—no annoying itch! For end consumers, the product offers the same insulation benefits as traditional insulation but has a range of indoor air-quality benefits—all while being price competitive. And the company saves a bunch on the raw material efficiency while also offering a product with many additional unique benefits at the same price as mainstream competitors. That is a way to win!

Knauf Insulation is no less resourceful on the process side. At the glass mineral wool production sites, the company developed pathways to reuse both production- and office-generated waste. Baled glass wool waste is reused as raw material by a ceiling tile manufacturer. Mixed-glass wool and related packaging waste is reprocessed for use as bedding for buildings and underground transit. At Knauf Insulation's extruded polystyrene (XPS) facility in Hartlepool, England, all manu-facturing waste is brought back into the production process—general and kitchen waste is picked up by a waste-management partner com-pany. To allow for any excess material to be fed back into the manu-facturing process, the company recently built its own recycling facility. To ensure capacity utilization and cost efficiency for raw materials, the company has made agreements with key customers for them to return their waste so that it can be reused, therefore improving the life-cycle performance of Knauf Insulation's products. Knauf Insulation also found a way to partner with a local community-interest company, donating waste materials such as cardboard to be reused as low-cost arts and crafts resources for community centers, colleges, and schools.

Knauf Insulation is a perfect example of a company using the principles of the Overfished Ocean Strategy—and winning with them. But the question here is not what it does, but how it got there. Anyone who's familiar with "KI" is aware of the strong imprint of its inspir-ing CEO, Tony Robson, well supported by his strategic marketing and manufacturing teams.

Was there another department involved?

It turns out, there was. An HR department, to be precise.

A few years ago, I got an unexpected call. Patrice Briol, group HR director of Knauf Insulation, read something about my work in an in-flight magazine (of all places!) and wanted to find a way for us to work together. His take on the issue, however, was rather unusual: instead of focusing on a specific department or function, he wanted to embed new thinking throughout the entire company and use the forces of all HR professionals in the company as a starting point.

After weeks of discussions and e-mail exchanges, we met in Brussels at a gathering of the company's HR professionals, with great number of executives from other functions joining the meeting. To set the stage and build a business case, Patrice put on a video. No, he was not showcasing 100 ways to turn "green" into gold. On the screen, author Dan Pink was talking about the science of human motivation.

"Contingent motivators—if you do this, then you get that—work in some circumstances. But for a lot of tasks, they actually either don't work, or, often, they do harm. This is one of the most robust findings in social science, and also one of the most ignored." On the stage of TEDGlobal 2009, Pink seemed determined to set the record straight.

Working on his 2011 book, *Drive*, Pink spent a number of years researching and analyzing the science of human motivation. At the center of his quest was a simple question: what works better—intrinsic motivators, which come from inside a person and require validation of no one, or extrinsic motivators, the carrots and sticks offered by other people?

Pink's conclusion was rather loud and clear: there is a great wall between science and business, where managers and companies consistently ignored hundreds of experiments run in different contexts, economies, and organizations. Essentially, business has made its biggest bet on extrinsic motivators—bonuses, awards, corner offices, and parking spots—in an attempt to secure the highest levels of performance. Yet experiment after experiment in both affluent and emerging societies shows that if-then rewards, the carrots and sticks, work only for a rather narrow set of circumstances. Extrinsic motivators bring about a high level of performance where there is a clear goal and a simple set of rules for getting there. Rewards and bonuses act as a focusing mechanism, narrowing our attention, allowing us to quickly zoom to the finish line.

But for a task that has any level of complexity, uncertainty, and innovation built into it, extrinsic motivators do not work. The reason, Pink clarifies, is very important: here, solutions are not obvious and the steps are blurry. To discover the right path, you cannot focus on one item—rather, look around, explore the periphery, open up your possibilities. Awards and bonuses do the exact opposite.

Extrinsic and intrinsic motivators are often confused: it is assumed that people who feel motivated perform better—so we need to build up energy and a sense of motivation with some clearly defined reward. But that is not what the science shows. Pink illustrates:

> Dan Ariely—one of the great economists of our time—he and three colleagues did a study of some MIT students. They gave these students a bunch of games that involved creativity and motor skills and concentration. And they offered them, for performance, three levels of rewards: small reward, medium reward, large reward. If you do really well, you get the large reward, on down. What happened? As long as the task involved only mechanical skill, bonuses worked as they would be expected to: the higher the pay, the better the performance. OK? But when the task called for even rudimentary cognitive skill, a larger reward led to poorer performance.[8]

To take into account the possible cultural bias and different levels of affluence, the researchers decided to repeat the experiments in Madurai, India, where the standards of living are much lower and rewards, relatively small by North American standards, would be considered much more substantial. The set-up was exactly the same: a number of games and three levels of rewards to drive higher performance. To much of my, Pink's, and hopefully your surprise, this time people who were offered the highest level of reward performed worse of all. "In eight of the nine tasks we examined across three experiments, higher incentives led to worse performance."[9]

When we use traditional extrinsic motivators—rewards, bonuses, titles—instead of intrinsic motivators, our teams might feel better. They might exude more energy. They might spill over with enthusiasm. But they do worse. When compared with less-known intrinsic motivators—a sense of purpose, a quest for learning, a feeling of freedom—extrinsic motivators lose more often than we think. And failure of extrinsic motivators is exactly what Patrice Briol and his HR department at Knauf Insulation wanted to take on. Their hypothesis? That the survival of the company depended on its ability to sustain and prosper despite the rapidly disappearing resources and the aftermath of the 2008 economic crisis. Such survival was a complex and challenging task. And this challenge might just be the intrinsic motivator that the entire company would benefit from. It was time to develop a new mind-set for a new challenge!

Instead of adding a new department to Knauf Insulation's corporate structure, the HR team decided to add a range of new competencies to be mastered by all employees—and managed by all with a range of tools, such as the company's 360-degree feedback program, which captures information all around about a person's performance. Each of the competencies was expressed in specific behaviors, which were easy to understand, easy to develop, and easy to manage—all contributing to the development of a new way of thinking and working. It was time to move *from department to mind-set.*

Overfished Ocean Strategy: The Winning Mind-Set

The mind-set required for development and execution of a successful Overfished Ocean Strategy is built on a range of distinct capabilities—and the particular winning cocktail of competencies depends on your company, your industry, and your reality. Yes, the trusted aptitudes of the corporate world, often referred to as left-brain capabilities,[10] are still in the game: we continue to need solid analysis, precise measurement, and disciplined execution. Yet as I have been pushing and pulling and nagging through the previous chapters, these staples of business success are simply not enough. A new set of competencies, more often associated with the right-brain world of artists, inventors, and "cultural creatives,"[11] is required for the unexpected, complex, and messy challenges of navigating the path *from line to circle*. While we have already discussed some of these competencies and skills, others are missing and deserve particular attention:

- *Systems thinking*—which focuses on how things interact within a whole—allows you and your team to manage and change at the scale of the entire value chain, rather than being stuck with dispersed, disconnected, and useless pieces of your puzzle. Like many other forms of thinking, systems thinking can be acquired and mastered. A close kin of systems thinking is *transdisciplinarity*—first developed as a research approach—which can be applied to business practices and processes. Companies have used cross-functional teams, job shadowing, rotations, and horizontal promotions as ways to strengthen transdisciplinary and holistic thinking within the company. Much more is needed.

- *Stakeholder management* particularly comes in handy as you begin your transformation *from line to circle* and *from a vertical to a horizontal* orientation—as it is likely that you will discover yourself in relationship with people and organizations you never thought existed. Suppliers of suppliers of suppliers, community leaders halfway across the world, customers you did not know you had, competitors you can benefit from, legislators who need your help . . . the list is long. The same applies to internal stakeholders of every kind—your counterparts throughout your company. The art of *influence*—of selling your ideas—is key.

- *Design thinking* has become the latest "it" tool for any respectable businessperson to conquer—and for a good reason. Unlike the decision mind-set—the most used managerial tool, which is all about making a hard choice between easy-to-identify alternatives—design thinking assumes an easy choice between difficult-to-create alternatives.[12] Tim Brown, CEO and president of IDEO, ranked among the 10 most innovative companies in the world, illustrates this new reality in the following way: "A management philosophy based only on selecting from existing strategies is likely to be overwhelmed by new developments at home and abroad. What we need are new choices—new products that balance the needs of individuals and of society as a whole; new ideas that tackle the global challenges of health, poverty, and education; new strategies that result in differences that matter and a sense of purpose that engages everyone affected by them. What we need is an approach to innovation that is powerful, effective, and broadly accessible. Design thinking . . . offers just such an approach."[13]

I will stop here to avoid the risk of killing any desire for transformation you might still have after countless pages, and will offer a few references that might help you as you move *from department to mindset* and start winning with it.

Building Your Tool Kit

In the previous chapters, we have covered most of the competencies needed to save the Overfished Ocean Strategy from a department prison and turn it into a powerful mind-set energizing the entire organization, so there is no point in listing all of the resources proposed for your tool kit up to this point. Here are a few additions you might find particularly handy:

- While there are many academic books on *stakeholder management*, very few of them are written for a typical (busy and slightly cynical, forgive my bluntness) manager. In essence, stakeholder management is about influence—the ability to sell your ideas and collaborate across all kinds of divides. The three best books on the topic, as I see it, are *To Sell Is Human: The Surprising Truth About Moving Others*, by my enduring favorite, Daniel H. Pink (New York: Riverhead Books, 2012); *The Five Dysfunctions of a Team: A Leadership Fable*, by Patrick Lencioni (San Francisco: Jossey-Bass, 2002), which gained a faithful following around the globe; and *Influence: The Psychology of Persuasion*, by Robert B. Cialdini (New York: HarperBusiness, 2006).

- *Design thinking* has recently exploded with countless books to choose from and many more resources to explore. The favorite— and most practical, in my view—is *Change by Design: How Design Thinking Transforms Organizations and Inspires Innovation*, by Tim Brown of IDEO. IDEO started with traditional design (e.g., design of objects) but soon after found itself in a broader field of innovation—inventing business models, user experiences, and entire organizations. You can start exploring Tim Brown's work at http://designthinking.ideo.com/.

- The topic of the uncertain future has been explored in many think tanks, and it might be helpful to track their research on the skills we will need to ride through the rough waters. Institute for the Future (IFTF) is just one such institution, and its *Future Work Skills 2020* report describes such capabilities as "Novel and Adaptive Thinking—proficiency at thinking and coming up with solutions and responses beyond that which is rote or rule-based" and "Social Intelligence—ability to connect to others in a deep and direct way, to sense and stimulate reactions and desired interactions." The entire report is available at http://www.iftf.org /our-work/global-landscape/work/future-work-skills-2020/.

———

We have traveled a long journey together—from an exploration of the marketplace to the discovery of the five principles that make up the emerging Overfished Ocean Strategy. The only question that remains here is where to start—or what, exactly, should your steps toward resource-intelligent innovation be? What should business do?

Over the past few years, I have watched companies of every size, geography, and industry answer this question in very different ways. Some got it right. Many got it wrong. So to answer the essential question of what business should do, we must first turn our attention to what, as I see it, most businesses should *not* do. It is my hope that by the end of the next chapter, we can all declare that green is dead. But the key question here is this: Is your marriage sustainable?

CHAPTER 8

The Death of Green, or
Is Your Marriage Sustainable?

AT A GLANCE

THE GLOBAL "GREEN" MOVEMENT has offered many solutions for the growing resources crunch. Many companies already have sustainability projects and green products. Why invent another strategy?

Once upon a time, there was a group of change makers that, it seemed, had figured it all out. Long before the awakening of the majority, this tiny minority saw the overfishing of the ocean at a distance and decided to act on it. They took on the challenge of the disappearing economy to a new level and attacked it head-on with new products, new processes, and new services. They wrote numerous books and spoke at many conferences. They pushed for industry-wide changes and gave birth to one unified answer to the resource challenge: the "green" economy.

I used to be one of them.

"Used to" is the crucial element here. For over a decade, I worked with countless companies on a range of sustainability risks and wrote articles and books on how to turn them into opportunities. All those years, it was a real pleasure and honor to work on projects that were much more than skin deep. Like many of you, I watched the rise in importance of everything "green" in media of every kind and attended the never-ending list of events that all seemed to suggest that "green" was the new black. The companies were courageous, the projects had impact, and the discoveries were potent. Yet in the bigger scheme of things, I could barely see any change in the mind-sets, behaviors, and outputs of the majority of companies worldwide. Green—as the answer to the challenge of the overfished oceans—was not working. Increasingly, something simply did not add up.

———

What comes to mind when you hear the phrase "green product"? Let's make it a bit more tangible. Imagine an "eco-shoe" . . . what do you see?

Most likely, some ecologically sound raw materials would come to mind—recycled or biodegradable, organic or nontoxic. Would this product be beautiful, aesthetically pleasing? When I ask this question at conferences, executive education sessions, and company meetings, most people shake their heads in an emphatic no. What about functionality—would it perform on par with a traditional shoe and have as much research built into it? Again, most people don't think so. And what about the price? Here we also have an agreement: green products are expected to cost more. The outrageously pricey organic lipstick that runs down your face in five minutes, the green car of the future that would hardly claim a proud spot in the owner's garage, a sad-looking organic apple twice the price of its conventional counterpart—the list goes on. If we sum it up, in the eyes of an average consumer, green products are ugly, underperform, and are expensive. Why in the world would we ever think that somebody is there to buy them?

The myth of "green" has been spreading like wildfire with the helping hand of marketing research. As far back as 2006, a National Consumers League and Fleishman-Hillard survey of US consumers reported the social responsibility of a company as being the number-one determining factor of brand loyalty, with 35 percent of respondents placing it on top, well ahead of product price and availability, each of those receiving a bare 20 percent of respondents' votes. Three years later, Deloitte reported that while much of consumer behavior was still dictated by price, quality, and convenience, a whopping 95 percent of American consumers said that they were willing to "buy green,"[1] while a BBMG survey[2] that combined a national poll of 2,000 consumers with ethnographic interviews supported the Deloitte findings: nearly 7 in 10 Americans (67 percent) agreed that "even in tough economic times, it is important to purchase products with social and environmental benefits." A year later, it became clear that concerns for the environment were not limited to the consumers from developed economies—the 2010 World Economic Forum report suggested that such concern was as strong in the emerging economies as well, "and in some areas stronger as they are often more directly affected, for example water pollution."[3] Sounds convincing, right?

The trouble in the research paradise started showing up when the announced "willingness to pay," as economists call it, failed to realize in practice. Customers promised one thing and did another. Take, for example, public utility. Despite strong support for the "green electricity" idea in consumer polls, few utility companies have been able to attract any significant consumer following once the product was offered. The story of Massachusetts's public utilities is a perfect illustration of this phenomenon. Massachusetts' electric utilities have offered programs like National Grid's GreenUp that let customers choose clean-energy sources for their power supply, for a premium. But in spite of an extensive marketing campaign, which included putting inserts in bills, sending online newsletters, hosting booths at events, and posting on Facebook to promote the options, there have been few takers. Barely 6,000 of the 1.2 million Massachusetts customers, or less than *half of 1 percent*, have signed up for GreenUp.[4] It turns out people do what they do, not what they say. Surprised?

In their painful discovery, Massachusetts's electric utilities were not alone. For a number of years, market data and academic research alike have signaled that the prevailing idea of green is dead. In a 2011 *Forbes* magazine article, Gregory Unruh puts it this way:

> Consumers and the public . . . expect sustainability as a baseline condition of business. They don't expect to pay for it. . . . Green marketers have known this for a long time. Consumers will consistently tell surveys that they are willing to pay more for socially and environmentally superior products. But when they are alone in the shopping aisle . . . , they rarely fork out more for "green." . . . It's a problem that established companies face when they add a new sustainable product to the portfolio. It immediately prompts the question "Well if this new product's green, what does that say about the rest of your line?"[5]

Many corporate executives see this response as a slap in the face for taking the path toward sustainability. They are, in a way, being punished for going green.

In 2010, four professors from Villanova University and SUNY Albany discovered during the course of their research that even financial markets are willing to punish for sustainability misdoings while they balk at paying a premium for going green.[6] The researchers found that being listed on a sustainability index doesn't improve share prices. However, when a company is thrown out from the index, the market inflicts a strong punishment—an average 1.2 percent of share-price loss following the delisting.

Consumer and market research has consistently confirmed academic research of this kind: Trendwatching.com put the death of green as one of its 11 most important trends for 2011, speaking of the plateauing number of consumers searching for "green" products, with the mainstream starting to question the value of going green:

- While 40 percent of consumers say they are willing to purchase green products, only 4 percent of consumers actually do when given the choice. (Source: *Journal of Marketing*, September 2010.)

- Fifty-eight percent of global consumers think that environmentally friendly products are too expensive, while 33 percent of global consumers think that environmentally friendly products don't work as well. (Source: GfK Roper, September 2010.)

- While the volume of green products available to US consumers increased by 73 percent between 2009 and 2010, only 5 percent of products were not found to include some "greenwashing" claims. (Source: Terrachoice, October 2010.)[7]

Greenwashing—a practice of deceptively spinning data to create the perception of an environmentally and socially friendly company—has been a fertile ground for mistrust and aversion to green, which seemed to grow through 2010 and 2011. Data from 2012 is even more worrisome. An *Advertising Age* headline says it all: "As More Marketers Go Green, Fewer Consumers Willing to Pay For It." What the magazine is referring to is the surprising results of the annual Green Gauge survey by GfK suggesting that while 93 percent of consumers reported they had personally changed their behavior to be more into conservation, they were becoming less willing to pay extra for green products.

> The survey of 2,000 US consumers, fielded last summer, finds five- to 12-point drops in the percentage of consumers willing to pay more for eco-friendly cars, biodegradable plastic packaging, energy-efficient light bulbs, electricity from renewable resources, or clothing made of organic or recycled materials. Much of the fault for the consumer pushback lies with marketers for over-hyping green products and making overly aggressive claims. "You have this kind of heightened distrust," said Diane Crispell, consulting director at GfK. "Consumers have become hypercritical. You see it with green and health claims."[8]

That is exactly why Volkswagen decided *not* to sell its Golf TDI BlueMotion in the United States. At 106 mpg, the car is a beacon of efficiency and eco-friendliness. Yet VW sees more potential in Europe, "where gas prices are double those in America, because consumers are more willing to pay up front for efficiency."[9] Green is dead?!

There is no question that my portrayal of the green economy is oversimplified, generalized, and exaggerated. It is also very clear that the challenges that the vast majority of green products are trying to address are very real, worthy, and urgent. But if, with the help of bad marketing, "green" has become synonymous with overpriced, over-hyped, half-baked products, that kind of green deserves to die. Simply put, no market exists for such products. Even more so, this approach undermines consumer trust and kills the chances for any kind of green to be successful. Environmentalists, who for a long time paid attention to environmental sustainability at the expense of financial sustainability, have to learn a hard lesson: both are necessary. Gernot Wagner, an economist and author at the Environmental Defense Fund, made this point into a powerful plea: "Don't stop recycling. Don't stop buying local. But add mastering some basic economics to your to-do list. Our future will be largely determined by our ability to admit the need to end planetary socialism (where the entire society pays for the actions of individual consumers). That's the most fundamental of economics lessons and one any serious environmentalist ought to heed."

Clearly, not all companies deal with the resource crunch in the same way. Throughout the first decade of the 21st century, as mainstream attempts at green started showing the fundamental flaw of placing a premium on the environmental, health, and social performance of business, a new wave of solutions appeared. A significant number of pioneering companies realized that it was time to put the existing green tactics to well-deserved rest and build an entirely new approach. And for a while, it seemed to be enough.

AFTER ALL, SUSTAINABILITY MEANS running the global environment—Earth Inc.—like a corporation: with depreciation, amortization, and maintenance accounts. In other words, keeping the asset whole, rather than undermining your natural capital.

MAURICE STRONG
ENTREPRENEUR AND FORMER UNDERSECRETARY-
GENERAL OF THE UNITED NATIONS

From Bolt-On to Embedded Sustainability

It was the fall of 2009, and amid the raging economic crisis, Chris Laszlo and I were as busy as ever. Chris, a friend, a former LaFarge executive, author of an outstanding list of books, and sustainability strategist extraordinaire, had been my partner on a number of projects and a real source of practical inspiration. That fall, we got together to share what was happening in our respective fields of work, as projects seemed to grow in size, number, and complexity. After a few days of heated debates, our consensus was palpable: something was shifting. We just needed to put our finger on it.

One intense year of research and practice later, the initial hunch had grown into a new framework, a body of writing to guide our work. It was clear: what was happening behind the closed doors of the most innovative companies worldwide was a significant transition in managing social and environmental risks. We saw this transformation as a move from "bolt-on" to "embedded" sustainability. Here was the best way we could make sense of this transition: what the small army of managers practicing the "green at a premium" format were doing, in essence, was simply "bolting on" social and environmental efforts to the existing strategy and operations, leaving them to hang there as a barely relevant appendix or a poorly fitted Band-Aid. But a handful of managers were doing something different: choosing to embed sustainability into the very DNA of what they did, incorporating environmental, health, and social value into core business activities with no trade-offs in price or quality. The Nissan Leaf, for example, a 100 percent electric car named World Car of the Year 2011, offered features at a price found on most gasoline-powered cars. Combined with the emerging infrastructure to recharge electric cars, Nissan's multibillion-dollar investment was driven by the quest for industry leadership and mainstream customer buy-in, not selling eco-cars to environmentalists. Leading companies such as Unilever, General Electric, and Erste Bank shared Nissan's approach, which goes beyond green.

Unlike the omnipresent bolt-on efforts, embedded sustainability requires a fundamental shift across every dimension of the business system.

In essence, what the pioneering companies figured out was that the most productive way to move forward with social and environmental pressure on business is to stop fighting and rather turn these demands

Table 1. Bolt-on versus embedded sustainability: key dimensions.

	Bolt-On Sustainability	Embedded Sustainability
Goal	Pursue shareholder value	Pursue sustainable value
Scope	Add symbolic wins at the margins	Transform core business activities
Customer	Offer "green" and "socially responsible" products at premium prices or with diminished quality	Offer "smarter" solutions with no trade-off in quality and no social or green premium
Value chain	Manage company's own activities	Manage across the product or service life-cycle value chain
Organization	Create a "scapegoat" department of sustainability	Make sustainability everyone's job

You can find this and many more concepts in the book I coauthored with Chris Laszlo in 2011, titled Embedded Sustainability: The Next Big Competitive Advantage. *I am thankful to Greenleaf Publishing and Stanford University Press for their permission to use it here.*

into a strategic advantage. The secret is integrating a new mind-set—a new way of looking at things—into all stages of company life, which in turn allows you to invent solutions without a quality compromise or green premium. Quite the contrary, embedded sustainability solutions are designed to drive down the costs or attract new revenues, making companies even more competitive. Sounds good, doesn't it?

Yes, it does. The concept of embedded sustainability continues to serve me—along with many companies around the world!—and I stand by the spirit of this work. For the vast majority of companies that took it on board, embedded sustainability brought about real results, driving profits and mitigating risks. The problem is, there are just too few such companies around. After decades of powerful discussions and endless developments on the why, the what, and the how of sustainability in business, the concept is still not embedded in the minds of even a small portion of managers in the world. What is going on here?

It's All About My Marriage

I have been working at the intersection of strategy, change management, and sustainability for nearly 15 years. Most of the time, my job has been to help companies with strategic risks and opportunities stemming from the declining resources, which, in turn, have led to new expectations from consumers, investors, regulators, and the public at large, all happening in the context of radical social media–fueled transparency. You would think that in the course of 15 years, this job would have become easier. Yet that is hardly the case: today, managers meet me with the same amazing mix of horror and boredom in their eyes as they did a decade ago. And when I ask my executive audiences to imagine being invited to a meeting about their company's sustainability strategy, the comments are consistent across the globe: such meetings are always a pain to endure.

Why do we have to go to such great lengths to explain and convince, excite and activate, business leaders' desire to work on managing ever-growing sustainability risks and opportunities? What is it that makes this so hard to swallow? Is it the fatigue and intellectual allergy to one more hyped-up management trend? Or is there something deeper? These questions were driving me crazy for a number of years—until one day at a management gathering, an amazing scene made the answer painfully clear. So let me set it up for you.

Imagine that you are having a wonderful dinner at your favorite restaurant. The night is great, the food is inspiring, the company is pure joy. On the way out, you bump into a former neighbor of yours—a great guy you shared beers and football talks with. You exchange pleasantries and a few updates about life and work. "How's your marriage?" you ask amid the flowing conversation. "Sustainable" comes the answer.

Smiling now, aren't you? So what is this smile about?

Sustainability, as a word in the English language, can hardly claim a place on the list of the most energizing and positive concepts around. It is simply not a good vision to strive for, as reaching sustainability does not make for a great achievement. We do not want marriages that are only sustainable. Similarly, building companies and societies that are merely sustainable is simply not good enough. We crave a much more powerful and captivating vision.

No wonder our managers are having trouble getting excited about it. The failure of the green movement to inspire and capture the minds of the business majority can be explained by poorly thought-out products and services. Yet even if all the troubles we explored with our eco-shoe discussion went away, the issue of language would be here to stay. Sustainability is simply not powerful enough. Our marriages, our companies, and our communities are better than that. We need an entirely new language—one that reflects an entirely new economy emerging right before our eyes. And that language is already here, moving beyond green into a much more alluring territory.

From Green to Smart

While green is dying and sustainability is struggling to inspire, something much deeper and more fundamental is happening in the market. As the rules of competition are beginning to shift, so are the winning strategies. As companies approach their products, services, and processes, a new way of thinking produces new results. You don't see a lot of it, but the stirrings are frequent enough and striking enough to suggest that something entirely new is ready to be born. The sprouts are everywhere. Puma, Tennant, and SeeChange Health are among them.

Remember the eco-shoe we met at the beginning of the chapter? Here is a completely different take on the same industry. When Puma, a German multinational beloved for its athletic wear, went out of its way to create a new, more resource-intelligent package for its shoes, it did not call it "green"—or "ecological," for that matter. The Clever Little Bag is a different kind of packaging that protects the shoes while doubling as a reusable shopping bag. The logic was simple: why do we expend a significant amount of paper for a shoe box; ship it to the store, where it is put into even more paper—the shopping bag; and then see it all in the trash only a few minutes after the purchase makes it home? Is there a more intelligent way? It turns out there is!

The goal was simple: Puma was going for nothing less than the smartest shoebox in the world. It partnered with design studio FuseProject and spent 21 months to develop a complete understanding of the entire value chain, generate over 2,000 ideas, observe factory behaviors all around the globe, and produce more than 40 packaging prototypes, all with the goal of reducing material and fabrication costs. The result was a new concept in packaging—a bag you can use again and again.

The Clever Little Bag delivers value to the company by protecting the shoes during transportation and storage—and also delivers an add-on value to the customer by offering a reusable bag to take to

Figure 7. Puma's Clever Little Bag goes from green to smart.

school or store the shoes in. The bag requires 65 percent less paper to produce when compared with the original packaging; reduces water, energy, and diesel consumption in manufacturing by over 60 percent; and cuts CO_2 emissions by 10,000 tons a year. As a smart product, it is beautiful, functional, and cheap, all at once. Moreover, it is a remarkably efficient marketing device. "If the packaging is so smart," an average shopper might reason, "imagine what's inside."

———————

Founded in 1870, Tennant Company, for much of its existence, had completely ignored resource depletion and other environmental considerations related to its products and operations as a factor of competitive differentiation. For the Minneapolis-based producer of floor-cleaning equipment and technologies, it all changed in 2002, when Chris Killingstad, the company's CEO, attended one of his first trade shows that year: "When I walked into the room, I saw hundreds of different machines that looked exactly the same, except for their colors. I realized that we had to do something to differentiate ourselves." In the mind of the company leadership, the global resource crunch emerged as a clear opportunity; yet there was something particularly fresh in Tennant's approach. Killingstad puts it this way: "We will not skew to a Patagonia or Seventh Generation model. Our goal is not to fill a green or eco niche; it's about achieving profitable growth within the industry. We aspire to substantially grow our business. This will require continued innovation and the absence of trade-offs—in price or performance—for our customers."[10]

With the bar set so high, Tennant went about delivering a number of ingenious solutions, perfecting the process of innovation one product at a time. A real breakthrough came about when Tennant scientists traveled to Japan. Hospitals there had developed a way to turn ionized tap water into an effective sanitizing agent. When an oxygenation and electrolysis process was applied to tap water, the breakdown of the molecules created an acidic solution that could kill bacteria. When Tennant's scientists began to study this idea further, it turned out that the process produced a second by-product that acted as a strong cleaner. Violà—a chemical-free technology was born and disrupted the entire cleaning industry.

With the new approach, operators of cleaning equipment had only to put water in their tank and go. And at the end of the process, what was left to be thrown out was essentially only dirty tap water. Moreover, the new technology used water more efficiently, reducing water use by up to 70 percent, whereby the operator could fill up less often and clean faster. Not only did the process get easier, but also it reduced the amount of money customers spent on chemicals and related costs, such as the cost of training. It also did not leave any chemical residues on floors, greatly reducing the potential risk of slip-and-fall accidents—which accounted for around 20 percent of insurance costs in retail environments, suggesting an opportunity for cost savings for Tennant's clients.

Tennant introduced the new ec-H2O technology platform at an industry trade show in fall 2007. With multiple benefits for the cleaners and the users of cleaned surfaces (that would be all of us), the company has been enjoying steady growth in the revenues of ec-H2O, starting at $17 million in 2008 and jumping to $96 million in 2010 and beyond. That is taking it from green to smart!

————

What does a sane insurance company—or any company, for that matter—strive for, day after day? Selling more, indeed. Growth has become the mantra for any rational manager, programmed into our heads everywhere we turn, from classrooms to newsrooms to boardrooms. So why would you go out of your way to bring your *revenue per customer* down—encouraging, if not pushing, a growing list of discounts and perks on every consumer?

There is no question that SeeChange Health is not your regular company. SeeChange Health took the concept of *health* insurance on its face value—and started focusing on health. The result: careful design of "value-based benefits" for all employers offering health insurance. So where is the value? SeeChange Health's insurance aims to increase the health of employees, increase productivity for the employers, and decrease costs for everyone, by rewarding healthy actions with hefty financial returns. Less sickness means fewer materials and resources used for recovery—yet, somehow, less becomes more. *Fast Company* named SeeChange Health number 20 on its "The World's 50 Most Innovative Companies of 2013" list. Here is how the magazine's J. Lester Federer explains this choice:

> The simplest way to lower healthcare costs is also the hardest: encourage healthy behavior. That's the premise behind the insurance policies of SeeChange Health, which . . . offers customers many discounts—depending on how healthy any one person works to be. . . . Before selling its own policies in 2010, it managed plans for larger insurers (which it still does). In one case, it incentivized 45% of diabetics to drop an average of 9 pounds, which led to a 19% drop in costs over two years. The company is now adding 2,200 members per month. In 2012, it says revenue increased sevenfold, to $54.2 million. That's healthy growth.[11]

I'd say.

————

My favorite consumer-behavior wizard, Trendwatching.com, has been speaking about this new wave of products with relentless clarity since 2011: "When it comes to 'green consumption,' expect a rise in products that are not only eco-friendly, but superior to polluting incumbents in every possible way. Think a combination of eco-friendly yet superior functionality, superior design, and/or superior savings."[12]

Following this invitation, solutions similar to Puma's Clever Little Bag, Tennant's ec-H2O technology, and SeeChange Health's value-based insurance are sprouting up around the world, whispering of the new economy that is fighting to be born. The era of green is over. It is time to put niche green products and processes to much-deserved rest and start working on the new business-as-usual paradigm—finding remarkable win-wins in the process. It's time to discover—and benefit from—the Overfished Ocean Strategy. Our changing market and our society itself are simply no longer tolerant of anything less.

CHAPTER 9

As a Means of Conclusion: What Should Business Do?

AT A GLANCE

THEORY IS GREAT, BUT practice makes perfect. When it comes to the Overfished Ocean Strategy, how can a company go from theory to reality and power up innovation for a resource-deprived world? No shortcuts or cookie-cutter recipes: be prepared for a messy road ahead. Thankfully, it all starts with some very small steps.

So we made it. Walked through countless stories. Explored essential pieces of the Overfished Ocean Strategy puzzle. Made a few jokes. Now what?

Assuming that the ideas made sense and you are convinced that the Overfished Ocean Strategy is a must for your company, conventional wisdom dictates that it is time to start the change. And then manage it.

How to begin? Whether it is a dip in performance that drives our companies to embark on a grand change program, or pressure from legislators, consumers, or investors—whether it's inside out or outside in—it seems that all of us are expected to go through the same process. Step one: identify the problem. Step two: conduct a thorough root-cause analysis. Step three: brainstorm and analyze possible solutions. Step four: choose and develop a clear course of action. Step five: implement. Sounds easy, right?

I don't know about you, but I have yet to find a company where this perfect step-by-step plan ever worked. Yet we insist on taking this route again and again and again—and every time I ask a group of managers to draw me a change-management plan, they produce the same five steps. Perhaps that is exactly the reason why so many change efforts fail miserably. In 1996, in his blockbuster *Leading Change* (Boston: Harvard Business School Press), John P. Kotter revealed a shocking number: only 30 percent of change efforts succeed. Considering that change management was a very new discipline at that time, we can give it the benefit of the doubt; it had to have gotten better since then, right? Unfortunately, the progress was not visible. In 2008, a McKinsey survey of 3,199 executives around the world found, just as Kotter had, that only one transformation in three attempted succeeds.[1] How's that for change?

Albert Einstein once defined insanity as doing the same thing over and over again and expecting different results. At the cost of getting even crazier, I suggest that we look for an alternative course of action. And it has been hiding right under our eyes for a long time.

IDEAS ARE A COMMODITY. Execution of them is not.

MICHAEL DELL
DELL CHAIRMAN AND CEO

I said it before and I will say it again: modern management has
a thing for putting the world in boxes. We have discussed that in
depth—our narrow take on the vertical slice in a long horizon of the
value chain, our desire for neat controllable plans, and our obsessions
with departments and functions are all part of it. Managing strategic
change seems no different: we need clear, manageable steps—from
plan to implementation—and no other way will do. Yet the companies
I work with, manage, or own seem to live in a different universe—the
one that is messy, iterative, and full of happy (and devastating) accidents. We try things, before having any clue what the result might be,
and learn from our mistakes fast. And we go around in circles searching for new ideas, most of them showing up serendipitously, and not
because we planned them.

In essence, the Overfished Ocean Strategy breaks the expected
sequence of change management. Customarily, it is assumed that
you first develop the strategy and then implement it. In fact, the line
between strategy and execution has become so sharp that it is taken as
a sign of great wisdom to hear business leaders such as Jamie Dimon,
CEO of JPMorgan Chase, assert, "I'd rather have a first-rate execution
and second-rate strategy any time than a brilliant idea and mediocre
management."[2]

Yet for most of us who lived through at least one successful strategic management process, it is rather clear that the line, if it exists at
all, is less of a Great Wall of China and more of a jagged set of dots
guiding the ever-changing dance between strategy and execution.

Roger Martin, a strategy theorist and practicing manager, offered this passionate illustration in a 2010 *Harvard Business Review* article:

> If a strategy produces poor results, how can we argue that it is brilliant? It certainly is an odd definition of brilliance. A strategy's purpose is to generate positive results, and the strategy in question doesn't do that, yet it was brilliant? In what other field do we proclaim something to be brilliant that has failed miserably on its only attempt? A "brilliant" Broadway play that closes after one week? A "brilliant" political campaign that results in the other candidate winning? If we think about it, we must accept that the only strategy that can legitimately be called brilliant is one whose results are exemplary.[3]

Indeed, early successes with innovating for a resource-deprived world echoed Martin's strong questioning of the illusory line between strategy and execution. But even more so, they challenge the sequence of change itself. Every company I studied or worked with that dared to venture into the unknown terrain *from line to circle* had to do so in the nearly complete dark, each step suggesting the next, experimenting heavily, taking action courageously, and producing results long before a truly comprehensive strategy could be voiced. Long before it became clear what strategic pathways would take one from here to there, companies had to plunge into the first steps, reap the first low-hanging fruits, develop the first new capabilities, and survive the first failures. In other words, they had to learn their way into the Overfished Ocean Strategy.

———

"There are two people, and only two, whose ideas must be taught to every MBA in the world: Michael Porter and Henry Mintzberg. This was true more than 25 years ago, when I did my MBA at USC," said Karl Moore in a 2011 article in *Forbes*.[4] An outstanding teacher and writer himself, Moore has been fascinated with the two schools of strategic thought embodied by the two great individuals: Michael Porter, who advocates a more deliberate strategy approach, and Henry Mintzberg, who emphasizes emergent strategy. In light of the radical transformations our global economy has been going through lately, Moore asked himself a simple question: whose view on strategy is the most relevant today?

There is no question that the world of deliberate strategy has been occupying the world of classrooms and boardrooms alike for a long time. Thus, there is no surprise that Moore has plenty of strategic planning weekends spent in posh hotels to remind him of his days as a corporate manager at IBM. After a few days spent in the analysis of Porter's five forces, the group would usually end up with a pile of heavy binders—all working relatively OK in the 1980s and part of the 1990s as the way to use the past to predict the future.

But today, Moore argues, the world does not make such strategy easy to follow. The rapid rate of change, mixed with a range of cataclysmic events (the 2000s alone brought 9/11, SARS, hurricanes and tsunamis, global financial and economic crisis, the BP oil spill, and much more), requires a more adaptive, emergent approach to strategy. Mintzberg's emergent strategy offers exactly that: learning from practice, constantly adapting to and accommodating a changing reality, allowing for a pattern of actions to emerge. And therefore, for today's rapidly changing world, Moore finds emergent strategy ahead of the game:

> Porter's ideas are still relevant, my colleagues and I still teach them, . . . and when I talk to corporate CEOs they still use them as part of their strategy planning thinking. But they are getting a bit long in the tooth for today's different world. Henry's emergent strategy ideas simply seem to be more relevant to the world we live in today—they reflect the fact that our plans will fail. This is not to say that planning isn't useful, but other than some long term technology plans, the day of the 5 year and even 2 year plans has faded. . . . [S]trategic flexibility is what we are looking for in most industries.[5]

So much for a few clear steps to follow!

As this chapter concludes our journey through the Overfished Ocean Strategy, it would be entirely normal to expect (as a means of conclusion!) a clear set of tools and steps designed to guide you through the confusing and turbulent corridors of change—*from line to circle, from vertical to horizontal,* and on. Yet following the personal invitation of Henry Mintzberg to "learn our way into strategy," I discovered that no simple ready-made solutions would do you any good, as change of this magnitude is emerging, iterative, and messy. It turns out you cannot analyze your way into a new business model. You can only learn and innovate your way into it.

YOU CAN'T SIT ON the lid of progress. If you do, you will be blown to pieces.

HENRY J. KAISER
INDUSTRIALIST AND SHIPBUILDER

Powering Up (Small!) Innovation for a Resource-Deprived World

In our busy household, a typical Sunday is filled with arts and crafts. Papers are flying, beads are falling, colored paper gets stuck everywhere. Last week, I spent two hours cleaning yellow paint off the ceiling (don't ask!). Arts are us.

A few Sundays ago, while cleaning up, I picked up some pairs of scissors off the floor. One of them grabbed my attention. So I snapped a photo to contrast its uniqueness with a "normal" pair. Here it is.

Figure 8. Sometimes scissors can be smart as well as sharp.

The pair on the left is the regular kind: the same amount of material is used for both handles; metal serves as a base. But the pair on the right has something special: the part of the handle that does not sustain any pressure has no hard filler, just the soft wrapper that (as you can see) bends easily. This is a tiny change, almost hard to notice. But such a small improvement makes a big difference: it allows the scissors to become adjustable to different hands (so even a big hand can fit it) while saving a chunk of raw material for the producer. The consumer is happy while the company saves money. These scissors make my cut!

Whenever we talk about innovation, it is assumed that the product of the invention process has to be big. Breakthrough. Breathtaking. Yet the most potent and often most difficult type of innovation is the constant renewal that comes in small packages. Like removing a small portion of a handle on your favorite scissors. That takes a lot of skill.

And it is exactly where Overfished Ocean Strategy companies start with their journey. Experimentation—packaged in small portions, focused on quick wins and low-hanging fruit—is what allows you to make a lot of mistakes (safely!), train your eye to be able to notice the hidden value, and build the managerial muscles needed for this demanding transformation. And it just happens to be exactly what Walmart started with.

From its humble beginnings in 1962 to its present state as an international superpower, Walmart rightly claims the position of being one of the most renowned businesses worldwide. One might think that for a corporate superpower of such unlimited resources, innovation should be a natural aspect of daily life, whereby every possible discovery for a better business performance is made and implemented at the speed of light. Indeed, the company is well known for its outstanding practices in supply-chain and inventory management, where it has invented like no other. Yet one of its most recent waves of innovation came from the place least anticipated for an international giant.

In 2005, facing the pressures of declining resources and increasing demands, all fueled by increasing transparency, Walmart made its first official sustainability commitment by setting three specific goals:

- To be supplied 100 percent by renewable energy

- To create zero waste

- To sell products that sustain resources and the environment

Corresponding short-term goals were set in each category, such as "fleet 25 percent more efficient in three years" for the energy category and "25 percent reduction in solid waste in three years" for the waste category—all driving significant innovation wrapped in small packages. Rob Eldridge, then director of packaging trend and communication at Walmart, explained: "We realize that 'zero waste' is a very aggressive goal, but also realize that a lot of innovation is being driven as a result of that. The industry is coming to us with things they really never thought possible before. Through this we have identified more opportunities to reduce waste than I think we would have even imagined."[6]

So how did it work, exactly? With the goals set, it was time to experiment—searching for new ways of doing business that would allow for achievement of the tightly set requirements. One of Walmart's first experiments in the domain of zero waste was an effort to "right-size" the packaging for a private-label line of children's toys. For years, the cost-cutting champion followed the lead of its suppliers when selecting specific packages for the products sold in Walmart stores. The zero-waste goal created a new lens for assessing and making packaging decisions, driving a fundamental quest for reducing the packaging material. And with the new lens, it became apparent that some of Walmart's packages had room to spare; the product fit in a loose fashion, with some space left between the product and the package. Making the first step with just one of thousands of product lines, Walmart tested "right-sizing" for all 350 items in the product line. Shaving just about an inch (three to four centimeters) from each box in the line as well as master cartons, Walmart was able to save 3,425 tons of corrugated paper materials, 1,358 barrels of oil, 5,190 harvested trees, and 727 shipping containers, while creating savings of $3,540,000 in transportation costs in one year—an ultimate "aha!" moment for the accidental innovators.

———

It seemed to be a rather simple solution—just an inch off a box—but experiments similar to the one in the right-sizing story bring about a depth of discoveries. First, starting with "small" innovation trains your eyes to notice invisible risks and new opportunities. Second, countless examples show that even a rather timid transformation of this kind requires a significant mobilization of the company to drive changes in product design, production, packaging, supplier relations, and more. Doing it first at a relatively small scale allows you to learn from your own mistakes—in other words, to learn how to learn, faster. Third, a story of this kind quickly makes it through the corridors of the corporation, becoming fuel for the next wave of valuable discoveries. (As the example of Silicon Valley shows, one big success is enough to drive thousands more efforts.) The list goes on.

Give Me One Good Scenario

Starting a systematic search for low-hanging fruit is a great way to launch a wave of experiments with the Overfished Ocean Strategy. Another method that might get your inventive juices going is *scenario planning*.

Scenario planning (also known as scenario thinking or scenario analysis) has been around for decades. In business, no company made more out of it than Shell. Ever since the company started using different scenarios to imagine possible futures and adapt to them in the early 1970s, the practice of scenario planning has grown into a real art. The process, as Shell suggests, is deceptively simple:

> Shell Scenarios ask "what if?" questions to explore alternative views of the future and create plausible stories around them. They consider long-term trends in economics, energy supply and demand, geopolitical shifts and social change, as well as the motivating factors that drive change. In doing so, they help build visions of the future. . . . Organizations using scenarios find it easier to recognize impending disruptions in their own operating environment. . . . They also increase their resilience to sudden changes caused by unexpected crises like natural disasters or armed conflicts. In an industry often defined by uncertainty and volatility, Shell is stronger thanks to the forward planning capacity that scenarios bring.[7]

What happens to your business when the oil price hits $200 per barrel and stays there? Will your consumer base suffer if water is taxed? Are there changes to operations if weather-related damages increase multifold? The list of possible drivers of change is long, and scenario planning allows you to (a) define the most material of the risks, (b) brainstorm possible implications, and (c) imagine proactive responses to the future that might be. Scenario planning is not forecasting, so it is not about being spot-on but rather is about developing a new way of looking at things. And scenario planning allows you to speak about new possibilities without stepping on anybody's toes, so that the interdepartmental or interdivisional wars can be set aside as you explore *everybody's* future. That might just be a way to create one.

Overfished Ocean Strategy: A Few Closing Remarks

I started working on this book at exactly 3:18 p.m. on a cold February afternoon in the winter of 2012, standing in front of a group of executives, ready for my strategy talk. As I am writing these words, it is 2:22 p.m. on a warm August Tuesday, the cat is sleeping on the terrace, the year is 2013. In the course of one and a half years, countless companies took on countless projects demonstrating to me—and you—the path toward the Overfished Ocean Strategy. It seems that innovation for a resource-deprived world is gearing up.

For a world that is addicted to quick fixes, this book has none. It is, in the words of my dear friend and professor of leadership Jonathan Gosling, a very "slow fix." Instead of giving you clear rules and well-defined steps, I am here to speak about principles. I am convinced—judging by the pioneers in this field—that you are much better off developing your own rules of the game, creating your own unique business models, mixing up your own inimitable product cocktails.

The collapse of the linear throwaway economy is not a question of "if" but of "when." The change is coming, and the rapidly oscillating prices on everything from rice to gold are a first sign of the new reality. The question is, will you ride the high tides with mastery and purpose, or will you be swallowed by waves that are unexpected and unnoticed until it is too late? If the endless list of Overfished Ocean Strategy innovations is any indication, we should make it into the new world just fine. I am counting on seeing you there.

My Big Thanks

Writing a book is a deeply collaborative endeavor. It is a blissful storm of beautiful accidents that serendipitously show you the right direction. For *Overfished Ocean Strategy*, the first of these accidents happened when the team of 2degrees Network (a community of managers dedicated to "making sustainable business happen") asked me to write a series of blog posts for their site. One slow August morning, I decided to send this series to Jeevan Sivasubramaniam, the managing director of Berrett-Koehler Publishers. Jeevan nudged the idea further, asking Neal Maillet, the editorial director, to take a look at the text. Neal spent four long months working with me on every aspect of the book proposal and championing it within the BK editorial team. With this amazing care, the original idea I offered went through a fundamental transformation. Making this project relevant for mainstream business became my key task.

That transformation would have been impossible without another powerful nudge. Yevgeniy Feld, a commanding businessman and one of the most remarkable human beings I know, spent countless hours sharing with me how the world of investment works. Yevgeniy's strong convictions solidified my resolve to make a strategic framework that speaks to the reality of the global market, and I am deeply thankful for his care and honesty.

Once the initial idea grew into a solid book proposal, the Berrett-Koehler Editorial Board offered wonderful advice for making it work. At one of the discussions, Steve Piersanti, BK's president and publisher, suggested that I revise the book title. That is how *Overfished Ocean Strategy* got its name. To this day, the entire team at Berrett-Koehler Publishers and their partners continues to hold my hand and

171

walk me through every step, and I am ever more grateful and inspired by their professionalism, passion, and humanity. My big thanks go to Elissa Rabellino, who edited this text with great patience and care, and to Naomi Schiff, who led the entire design and production process.

While the book emerged in the course of a few months, the ideas presented here are built on the work of many demanding years and many extraordinary companies. I am grateful and honored to have a chance to share some of the stories of these pioneering enterprises, and my heartfelt thanks go to Dr. Thomas Becker, vice president government affairs, BMW Group; Patrice Briol, group HR director, Knauf Insulation; Sandi Cesko, cofounder and president, Studio Moderna; Jenniffer Deckard, CEO and president, Fairmount Minerals; Chuck Fowler, director and chairman of the Executive Committee, Fairmount Minerals; Mariana Gheorghe, CEO, OMV Petrom; Gerhard Roiss, chairman of the Executive Board and CEO of OMV Group; Iztok Seljak, president of the Management Board of Hidria; and Matevz Slokar, founder of S Project. Coca-Cola Company's continued support of my work and for me as the holder of the Coca-Cola Chair of Sustainable Development at IEDC-Bled School of Management is an amazing gift of intellectual freedom, and I extend big thanks to Muhtar Kent, chairman and CEO, and his entire team for this ongoing cooperation.

Many of the ideas presented here have been developed during executive education courses, conferences, summits, speeches, and unique global projects. I am forever indebted to these wonderful organizations and their inspiring leaders: the IEDC-Bled School of Management, particularly President and Dean Danica Purg and Academic Director Nenad Filipovic; the amazing and inspiring Challenge:Future community, and in particular its founder and president and a dear, immensely courageous friend, Andreja Kodrin; the Weatherhead School of Management at Case Western Reserve University, and particularly the Fowler Center for Sustainable Value, wonderfully led by my forever adored guides, mentors and teachers

David Cooperrider, Ron Fry, Chris Laszlo, and Roger Saillant and supported by the most amazing Advisory Board, which I am proud to be a member of; INSEAD-CEDEP, and in particular Director of General Management Programme Martin Flash; and the wonderful TEDx teams in Slovenia and Austria, with special thanks to Matej Golob.

Throughout the years, an amazing community of thinkers, colleagues, and friends has been supporting my life and work in many different ways. I am deeply grateful to Alibek Belyalov, Alena Chernenko, Dmitry Chernenko, Cristina Doros, Barbara Ferjan, Roman Finadeev, Ante Glavas, Lindsey Godwin, Jonathan Gosling, Maria Gudkova, Deniz Kirazci, Aleksandra Kosak, Marko Lucic, Yulia Mikina, Henry Mintzberg, Matthew Moehle, Yulia Oleinik, Aljaz Podlogar, Katalina Pojoga, Nicolae Pojoga, Niko Rakovec, Petra Rakovec, Alexey Redichev, Irina Redicheva, Linda Robson, Judy Rodgers, Natalia Sahanovschi-Iuras, Michael Uchitel, Olga Veligurska, my intellectual soul mates—the students and alumni of the doctorate program of the Organizational Behavior Department at Case Weatherhead—and the entire AYL crowd.

Finally, there is no way that I can find the right words to thank my family for everything that they are. As they graciously move through this turbulent life, every day they continue to show me what a life of courage and meaning really looks like. My gratitude and my love to all of you: Lidiya Zhexembayev, Timur Zhexembayev, Tatyana Nurgazina, Marat Zhexembayev, Olga Zhexembayeva, Alen Nurgazin, Iskander Nurgazin, Miras Nurgazin, Vladimir Zhexembayev, Irina Zhexembayeva, Enessa Gucker, Hans Gucker, Emma Jernovoi, and Slavyan Jernovoi (we really miss you!).

And there are two more. These amazing magicians endured my countless days of seclusion, served as hand models and photographers, debated key points, suffered through chapter readings, and held me together when all seemed useless. The two of them are my masters, my coaches, my most important benchmarks, my deepest reasons, my endless inspirations. To my husband, Vladimir Jernovoi, and daughter, Lila Jernovoi, I give my love and soul. Thank you.

Notes

Warm Greetings!

1. For more, see the in-depth McKinsey Global Institute & McKinsey Sustainability & Resource Productivity Practice report *Resource Revolution: Meeting the World's Energy, Materials, Food, and Water Needs*, November 2011, http://www.mckinsey.com/insights/energy_resources_materials /resource_revolution.

2. Kyle Wiens, "We're Running Out of Resources, and It's Going to Be OK," February 8, 2013, http://blogs.hbr.org/cs/2013/02/were_running_out_of _resources.html.

3. The work of Michael E. Porter, such as *Competitive Strategy: Techniques for Analyzing Industries and Competitors* (New York: The Free Press, 1998), is the best illustration of the positioning approach.

4. For more on this approach, see W. Chan Kim and Renée Mauborgne, *Blue Ocean Strategy: How to Create Uncontested Market Space and Make the Competition Irrelevant* (Boston: Harvard Business School Press, 2005).

Chapter 1. Where Are the Fish? The New Competitive Reality

1. See more on New England fish stock in David Ariosto, "Historic Cod Fishing Cuts Threaten Centuries-Old Industry in New England," CNN, February 4, 2013, http://www.cnn.com/2013/01/31/us/northeast-cod-fishing-cuts/.

2. Caroline Davies, "Study Suggests Decline in UK Fish Stocks More Severe Than Thought," *Guardian*, May 4, 2010, http://www.theguardian.com /environment/2010/may/04/fish-stocks-uk-decline.

3. See Stuart Biggs, Kanoko Matsuyama, and Frederik Balfour, "Tsunami Quickens 'Terminal Decline' of Northern Japan's Fishing Industry," *Bloomberg News*, April 25, 2011, http://www.bloomberg.com/news /2011-04-24/tsunami-speeds-terminal-decline-of-japan-s-fishing-industry .html.

4. See Denise Roland, "World Fish Stocks Declining Faster Than Feared," FT.com, September 28, 2012, http://www.ft.com/intl/cms/s/2/73d14032 -088e-11e2-b37e-00144feabdc0.html#axzz2Tg8ciFAK.

5. The full story on the wild fish can be found in David Biello, "Overfishing Could Take Seafood Off the Menu by 2048," *Scientific American*, November 2, 2006, http://www.scientificamerican.com/article.cfm?id=overfishing-could -take-se.

6. The Natural Step's website (http://www.naturalstep.org/) offers a number of free resources and tool kits.

7. See, for example, *The Dialogues of Plato*, edited and with an introduction by Erich Segal (New York: Bantam, 2006).

8. See Thomas Malthus's *An Essay on the Principle of Population* (Oxford: Oxford University Press, 2008, originally published in 1798).

9. McKinsey Global Institute, *Resource Revolution*, 21.

10. You can find this and much more excellent data in McKinsey Global Institute, *Resource Revolution*.

11. For this and much more data on energy, see BP, *Energy Outlook 2030*, January 2013, http://www.bp.com/en/global/corporate/about-bp/statistical-review -of-world-energy-2013/energy-outlook-2030.html.

12. We are grateful to Wikipedia for sharing this data, http://en.wikipedia.org /wiki/Price_of_petroleum.

13. CNN, "40% of US Food Wasted, Report Says," August 22, 2012, http://news .blogs.cnn.com/2012/08/22/40-of-u-s-food-wasted-report-says/.

14. Maps of World, "Top Ten Countries With Most Rice Producing Countries," http://www.mapsofworld.com/world-top-ten/rice-producing-countries.html.

15. Wikipedia, "2008 Global Rice Crisis," http://en.wikipedia.org/wiki /2008_global_rice_crisis.

16. D. R. Davis, M. D. Epp, and H. D. Riordan, "Changes in USDA Food Composition Data for 43 Garden Crops, 1950 to 1999," *Journal of the American College of Nutrition* 23, no. 6 (2004): 669–82.

17. Full details and the manual on the Global Water Footprint Standard can be found at Water Footprint Network, "Water Footprint," http://www .waterfootprint.org/?page=files/GlobalWaterFootprintStandard.

18. The World Water Council (http://www.worldwatercouncil.org) has plenty of current data.

19. Paul Bulcke, "Water—the Linchpin of Food Security," City Food Lecture, London, February 25, 2013, https://docs.google.com/file/d /0Bwx4b11cxeb2WmRfWDM3bHJfT1U/edit?pli=1.

20. Eduardo Porter, "For Insurers, No Doubts on Climate Change," *New York Times*, Business Day, May 14, 2013, http://www.nytimes.com/2013/05/15 /business/insurers-stray-from-the-conservative-line-on-climate-change .html?pagewanted=all&_r=0.

21. Bryan Walsh, "The Costs of Climate Change and Extreme Weather Are Passing the High-Water Mark," *Time*, July 17, 2013, http://science.time.com /2013/07/17/the-costs-of-climate-change-and-extreme-weather-are-passing -the-high-water-mark/.

22. Porter, "For Insurers, No Doubts on Climate Change."

23. Ruediger Kuehr and Eric Williams, eds., *Computers and the Environment: Understanding and Managing Their Impacts* (Dordrecht, the Netherlands: Kluwer Academic Publishers, 2003).

24. For more, see Verne Kopytoff, "The Complex Business of Recycling E-Waste," *Bloomberg Businessweek*, January 8, 2013, http://www.businessweek.com /articles/2013-01-08/the-complex-business-of-recycling-e-waste.

25. Andrew Grice, "UK Warned It Will Run Out of Landfill Sites in Eight Years," *Independent*, July 8, 2010, http://www.independent.co.uk/news/uk/home -news/uk-warned-it-will-run-out-of-landfill-sites-in-eight-years-2021136 .html.

26. Mohammed N Al Khan, "Dubai Running Out of Landfill Space to Dump Its Rubbish," *National*, September 23, 2012, http://www.thenational.ae/news /uae-news/dubai-running-out-of-landfill-space-to-dump-its-rubbish.

27. Marsha Walton, CNN science and technology producer, wrote about such fields in her post titled "The Pacific 'Toilet Bowl That Never Flushes,'" http://scitech.blogs.cnn.com/2008/08/13/the-pacific-toilet-bowl-that-never -flushes/.

28. See more on VC investment trends at PWC, "Venture Capital Investments Decline in Dollars and Deal Volume in Q1 2013, according to the Moneytree Report," April 19, 2013, http://www.pwc.com/us/en/press-releases/2013 /venture-capital-investments-decline-in-dollars.jhtml.

29. See Daniel Isenberg, "Enabling the Natural Act of Entrepreneurship," *Harvard Business Review*, April 10, 2013, http://blogs.hbr.org/cs/2013/04 /enabling_the_natural_act_of_en.html.

30. Sandi Cesko, remarks made at the conference "CSR: From Coincidence to Strategy," Bled, Slovenia, May 13, 2013.

31. Daniel H. Pink, *A Whole New Mind: Why Right-Brainers Will Rule the Future* (New York: Riverhead, 2005).

32. Rob Walker, "The Worm Turns," *New York Times Magazine*, May 20, 2007, http://www.nytimes.com/2007/05/20/magazine/20wwln-consumed-t.html ?_r=0.

33. More about the new mobility efforts of BMW can be found on the BMW i Mobility Services page, http://www.bmw.com/com/en/insights/corporation /bmwi/mobility_services.html#drivenow.

34. For Bloomberg's analysis of BMW's recent energy moves, see Stefan Nicola, "BMW Adds Wind Power to Sidestep Merkel's Power Bill," *Bloomberg*, February 19, 2013, http://www.bloomberg.com/news/2013-02-18/bmw -adds-wind-power-to-sidestep-merkel-s-power-bill.html.

35. Nelson D. Schwartz, "Swiss Re," CNNMoney, http://money.cnn.com /galleries/2007/fortune/0703/gallery.green_giants.fortune/9.html.

36. For more about Swiss Re and its climate change business, starting with the report on Andreas Spiegel's contribution to Bloomberg TV, see Swiss Re, "Swiss Re on Bloomberg TV: Insuring Climate Change," http://www.swissre .com/rethinking/insurers_and_climate.html.

Chapter 2. Overfished Ocean Strategy: Five Principles That Make It Work

1. For more on Michael Porter's work, see "Porter's Generic Strategies," Wikipedia, http://en.wikipedia.org/wiki/Porter's_generic_strategies.

2. Huawei is eager to go beyond its current market focus to capture the global market. For more, see Kristie Lu Stout, "Would You Buy a Huawei Smartphone?" CNN, May 16, 2013, http://edition.cnn.com/2013/05/09 /business/china-huawei-smartphones-stout.

3. I have borrowed these words of Clayton M. Christensen from a wonderful article by Larissa MacFarquhar, "When Giants Fail," *New Yorker*, May 14, 2012, http://www.newyorker.com/reporting/2012/05/14/120514fa_fact _macfarquhar. You can find much more of Christensen's powerful research in his own book *The Innovator's Dilemma: The Revolutionary Book That Will Change the Way You Do Business* (New York: HarperCollins, 2011, reprint edition).

4. For the story of the Lush solid bar development, see Lush, "What Do You Know About: Solid Shampoo?" https://www.lush.co.uk/content/view/994.

5. Christopher Muther, "Beauty Bet: Lush's Solid Shampoo," Boston.com, May 24, 2011, http://www.boston.com/lifestyle/fashion/stylephile/2011 /05/beauty_bet_lush.html.

6. Lush received an important award for the ingenious packaging of its solid shampoo; see RSA, "Lush 'Squeaky Green': Best Green Packaging Award," 2008, http://www.rsaaccreditation.org/index.php/green-awards-cs/98-lush -squeaky-green-best-green-packaging-award.

7. For the full story of Mark and Mo Constantine, the founders of Lush, see David Teather, "Lush Couple with a Shed Load of Ideas," *Guardian*, April 13, 2007, http://www.guardian.co.uk/business/2007/apr/13/retail2.

8. For an in-depth look at the OMV Resourcefulness approach, see OMV Group, http://www.omv.com/.

9. Eco-Superior was one of five trends described in Trendwatching.com's July/ August 2013 Trend Briefing, *Trends: Refreshed*, http://www.trendwatching .com/trends/pdf/2013-07%20TRENDS%20REFRESHED.pdf.

10. For more on the "Design Hotels is Finding Infinity" initiative, see "Finding a Future Based on Infinite Resources," Design Hotels, http://www.designhotels .com/specials/finding_infinity.

11. If *Blue Ocean Strategy* is new to you, you can start your exploration with *Blue Ocean Strategy*, Wikipedia, http://en.wikipedia.org/wiki/Blue_Ocean _Strategy.

12. The work of Michael E. Porter, such as *Competitive Strategy: Techniques for Analyzing Industries and Competitors* (New York: The Free Press, 1998), is the best illustration of the positioning approach.

13. For more on this approach, see W. Chan Kim and Renée Mauborgne, *Blue Ocean Strategy: How to Create Uncontested Market Space and Make Competition Irrelevant* (Boston: Harvard Business Review Press, 2004).

14. Michael Porter has advocated for the five forces analysis for a number of decades now; see "Porter Five Forces Analysis," Wikipedia, https://en .wikipedia.org/wiki/Porter_five_forces_analysis.

Chapter 3. Principle One: Line to Circle

1. All interviews for this story about Shaw Industries' EcoWorx invention were taped in 2004 for the production of a series of videos, which I oversaw as associate director of the Center for Business as an Agent of World Benefit at Weatherhead School of Management, Case Western Reserve University, Ohio. This center has since been renamed the Fowler Center for Sustainable Value, and I continue to proudly serve on its advisory board.

2. For an update on the EcoWorx story, see Shaw Contract Group, EcoWorx interactive brochure, http://www.shawcontractgroup.com/Content /LiteraturePDFs/Environmental_pdf/ecoworx_interactive.pdf.

3. This infographic by the *Guardian* and Accenture is a good introduction to the concept of circular economy. May 13, 2013, http://www.guardian.co .uk/sustainable-business/driving-circular-economy-infographic#zoomed -picture.

4. This number comes from the Ellen MacArthur Foundation, "Circular Economy Reports," http://www.ellenmacarthurfoundation.org/business /reports.

5. This quote appears at the opening of *Towards the Circular Economy, Vol. 2*, a project managed by McKinsey, a global consulting company, for the Ellen MacArthur Foundation, http://www.ellenmacarthurfoundation.org/business /reports/ce2013.

6. See "Cradle-to-cradle design," Wikipedia, http://en.wikipedia.org/wiki /Cradle_to_Cradle.

7. In Ellen MacArthur Foundation, "Cradle to Cradle—Products, but also Systems," case study, http://www.ellenmacarthurfoundation.org/circular -economy/circular-economy/part-v-in-reality-how-does-that-translate -the-ford-example.pdf.

8. See Phil Patton, "For Ford, a Green Roof That Springs Eternal," *New York Times*, December 29, 2010, http://wheels.blogs.nytimes.com/2010/12/29 /for-ford-a-green-roof-that-springs-eternal/?_r=0.

9. This and all other quotes from Paul Raines, along with the data about GameStop, are from Sean Hollister, "Recycled: Inside the GameStop Factory Where Gadgets Are Born Again," *Verge*, August 10, 2012, http://www.theverge .com/2012/8/10/3230609/gamestop-tour-interview-spawn-labs-paul-raines -tony-bartel.

10. Sean Hollister, "Recycled: Inside the GameStop Factory Where Gadgets Are Born Again," *Verge*, August 10, 2012, http://www.theverge.com/2012 /8/10/3230609/gamestop-tour-interview-spawn-labs-paul-raines-tony-bartel.

11. A great amount of detail about the FLOOW2 concept can be found in this case study by the Ellen MacArthur Foundation, http://www .ellenmacarthurfoundation.org/case_studies/floow2-1.

12. Trendwatching.com is one of the best sites to read about key consumer trends. For more on this particular trend, see "11. Owner-less," http://www .trendwatching.com/trends/11trends2011/#ownerless.

13. Bryan Walsh, "Today's Smart Choice: Don't Own. Share," *Time*, March 17, 2011, http://www.time.com/time/specials/packages/article /0,28804,2059521_2059717_2059710,00.html.

14. Katie Kramer, "Take a Seat with Rising Stars of the Sharing Economy," *Seat at the Table*, CNBC, http://www.cnbc.com/id/100668331.

15. Ellen MacArthur Foundation, *Towards the Circular Economy, Vol. 1*, http://www.ellenmacarthurfoundation.org/business/reports/ce2012.

16. The case of Kalundborg Industrial Symbiosis is described in a 2010 paper commissioned by the Nordic Council of Ministers, *Green Business Models in the Nordic Region—A key to promote sustainable growth*, http://w2l.dk/file/401339/fora-green-business-models.pdf. Additional data can be found in "One Man's Waste—Another Man's Gold," *Focus Denmark*, Special Issue 2011, http://www.symbiosis.dk/sites/default/files/DANISH%20EXPORT%20COUNCIL%20_FOCUS%20DENMARK%20_JUNE2011_KALUNDBORG_.pdf.

17. Jie Liu et al., "The Data Furnace: Heating Up with Cloud Computing," Microsoft Research, http://research.microsoft.com/pubs/150265/heating.pdf.

18. Ibid.

19. TerraCycle's business model depends on ground-up engagement and deep trust. The company makes all data about its operations available in real time online, along with all other practicalities of its operations; http://www.terracycle.com/en-US/.

20. For more about the HP Renew program and its trade-in offering, see HP Renew—Americas, "Success Stories," http://www.hp.com/united-states/renew/success-stories.html.

21. See Frost and Sullivan, *The Global Industrial Waste Recycling Markets*, https://tapahtumat.tekes.fi/uploads/c8ffe124/Tekes_GG_Workshop_021012_global_industrial_waste_presentation-9175.pdf.

22. For the full story of Coca-Cola Drink2Wear, see "Creating Value through Sustainable Fashion," January 1, 2012, http://www.coca-colacompany.com/stories/creating-value-through-sustainable-fashion.

Chapter 4. Principle Two: Vertical to Horizontal

1. See "Porter Five Forces Analysis," Wikipedia, https://en.wikipedia.org/wiki/Porter_five_forces_analysis.

2. See "Starbucks," Wikipedia, https://en.wikipedia.org/wiki/Starbucks.

3. The devastating impact of the coffee crisis is detailed in Fuzhi Cheng, "The Coffee Crisis: Is Fair Trade the Solution?" Food Policy for Developing Countries, http://cip.cornell.edu/DPubS/Repository/1.0/Disseminate?view=body&id=pdf_1&handle=dns.gfs/1200428207.

4. This quote, and all the background information on the Portland Roasting Company, comes from the 2010 teaching case titled "Portland Roasting Company: Farm Friendly Direct," by Madeleine Pullman, Greg Stokes, Price Gregory, Mark Langston, and Brandon Arends of Portland State University, http://www.sba.pdx.edu/cgls/media/Case%20Study%20-%20Portland %20Roasting%20FFD%20060410.pdf.

5. See "Resilient Supply Chain," Green Mountain Coffee roasters, http://www .gmcr.com/Sustainability/SupplyChain.aspx.

6. For GMCR financials, see "Investor Pages," http://investor.gmcr.com /financials.cfm.

7. See Madeline Pullman et al., "Portland Roasting Company: Farm Friendly Direct."

8. From David L. Cooperrider and Michelle McQuaid, "The Positive Arc of Systemic Strengths: How Appreciative Inquiry and Sustainable Designing Can Bring Out the Best in Human Systems," *Journal of Corporate Citizenship* 2012, no. 46 (June 2012): 71–102(32), http://www.ingentaconnect.com /content/glbj/jcc/2012/00002012/00000046/art00006.

9. Ibid.

10. Ibid.

11. From Sourcemap.com's "About" section, accessed January 2, 2014, http://free .sourcemap.com/info/about.

12. "Crowdsourcing," Wikipedia, http://www.wikipedia.org/wiki/Crowdsourcing.

13. Elise Ackerman, "Sourcemap, an MIT-Incubated Startup, Offers Solution to National Security Risk Posed by IT Supply Chain," *Forbes*, April 4, 2012, http://www.forbes.com/sites/eliseackerman/2012/04/04/sourcemap-an-mit -incubated-startup-offers-solution-to-national-security-risk-posed-by-it -supply-chain/.

14. Ibid.

15. See John Tozzi, Karen E. Klein, and Nick Leiber, "America's Most Promising Social Entrepreneurs," Sourcemap, *Bloomberg Businessweek*, June 21, 2012, http://images.businessweek.com/slideshows/2012-06-21/americas-most -promising-social-entrepreneurs-2012#slide21.

16. Robert G. Eccles and George Serafeim, "The Performance Frontier: Innovating for a Sustainable Strategy," *Harvard Business Review*, May 2013, http://hbr.org/2013/05/the-performance-frontier-innovating-for-a -sustainable-strategy/ar/1.

17. 100%Open, "Open Innovation Defined," http://www.100open.com/2011/03 /open-innovation-defined/.

Chapter 5. Principle Three: Growth to Growth

1. Sylvia Nasar, *Grand Pursuit: The Story of Economic Genius* (New York: Simon & Schuster, 2011).

2. From Keynes's toast on the occasion of his retirement from the *Economic Journal* in 1945, quoted in Roy Harrod, *The Life of John Maynard Keynes* (New York: W. W. Norton & Co., 1983).

3. Robert Nadeau, "The Economist Has No Clothes," *Scientific American*, March 25, 2008. http://www.scientificamerican.com/article.cfm?id=the -economist-has-no-clothes.

4. Ibid.

5. Rolls-Royce, "Rolls-Royce celebrates 50th anniversary of Power-by-the-Hour," October 30, 2012, http://www.rolls-royce.com/news/press_releases/2012 /121030_the_Hour.jsp.

6. For more about Volvo Aero, see Nordic Council of Ministers, *Green Business Models in the Nordic Region*, w2l.dk/file/401339/for a-green -business-models.pdf.

7. Charles Fishman, "Hire This Guy," *Fast Company*, November 2007, http:// www.fastcompany.com/60982/hire-guy.

8. Matevz Slokar, remarks made at the conference "CSR: From Coincidence to Strategy," Bled, Slovenia, May 13, 2013.

9. For more about the S Project, including Speak glass, see S Project, http:// sproject.org/. Up until July 2013, the site was in English; now it is in Slovene, but if you write to the founders, they do speak perfect English. Google Translate works well, too.

10. I had a number of conversations with Sandi Cesko over the course of the past several years, and these quotes come from remarks made via personal conversations, clarified via e-mails, and shared at common events. You can find many of the same ideas in Sandi Cesko's TEDxBled speech, available at http://www.youtube.com/watch?v=WRD0SXjRF8M.

11. Ibid.

12. For Simon Sinek's entire Tedx speech, see http://www.ted.com/talks/simon _sinek_how_great_leaders_inspire_action.html.

13. http://www.fastcodesign.com/1671633/how-to-think-about-turning-your -products-into-services.

14. B. Joseph Pine II and James H. Gilmore, "Welcome to the Experience Economy," *Harvard Business Review*, July 1998, http://hbr.org/1998/07 /welcome-to-the-experience-economy/.

Chapter 6. Principle Four: Plan to Model

1. For more about the Hidria Corporation, see http://www.hidria.com/.

2. This visual, along with much of the data used in this story, comes from Iztok Seljak's 2012 presentation to my Executive MBA class at IEDC-Bled School of Management, Slovenia.

3. For more about SiEVA, see http://www.sieva.si/en/about-sieva/introduction/.

4. For more about Feniks Consortium, see the organization's brochure, available at http://www.feniks-kg.com/material/brosura_eng_web.pdf.

5. This data comes from Jonathan Ablett, Lowell Bryan, and Sven Smit, "Anticipating Economic Headwinds," in the special report "Oil's Uncertain Future: What You Need to Know," *McKinsey Quarterly* 2011, no. 4.

6. The crowd-sourced work was published as a 2010 book, *Business Model Generation: A Handbook for Visionaries, Game Changers, and Challengers*, by Alexander Osterwalder and Yves Pigneur (New York: John Wiley & Sons), with 470 contributors.

7. For more about Safechem, see Tanja Bisgaard, Kristian Henriksen, Markus Bjerre, *Green Business Model Innovation,* Nordic Innovation, October 2012, http://www.nordicinnovation.org/Global/_Publications/Reports /2012/2012_12%20Green%20Business%20Model%20Innovation _Conceptualisation%20next%20practice%20and%20policy_web.pdf.

8. For more about Allfarveg, see Nordic Council of Ministers, *Green Business Models in the Nordic Region.*

9. For a brief history of lean manufacturing, see "Lean manufacturing," Wikipedia, http://en.wikipedia.org/wiki/Lean_manufacturing.

10. A PDF of the article can be downloaded from http://www.lean.org /downloads/MITSloan.pdf.

11. Steve Blank, "Why the Lean Start-Up Changes Everything," *Harvard Business Review*, May 2013, http://hbr.org/2013/05/why-the-lean-start-up-changes -everything.

12. This quote came from the homepage of the Lean Startup Movement, accessed January 13, 2014, http://theleanstartup.com/.

Chapter 7. Principle Five: Department to Mind-Set

1. Plato, *The Republic*, 2nd ed., reissued, trans. Desmond Lee (New York: Penguin Classics, 2003), 56.

2. For the origin of *department*, see Merriam-Webster, http://www.merriam -webster.com/dictionary/department?show=0&t=1387098631.

3. Max Weber's groundbreaking work on bureaucracy is described in many books and other sources. This quote is from http://pegasus.cc.ucf.edu /~janzb/courses/phi4804/weber1.htm.

4. Barry Schwartz, "Our Loss of Wisdom," TED talk, February 2009, http:// www.ted.com/talks/barry_schwartz_on_our_loss_of_wisdom.html.

5. Knauf Insulation, "Zero Waste to Landfill," July 31, 2013, http://www .knaufinsulation.com/en/content/zero-waste-landfill.

6. Knauf Insulation used this data in its 2012 *Sustainability Report*, http:// www.knaufinsulation.com/.

7. Knauf Insulation, *Knauf Insulation with ECOSE Technology*, http:// www.knaufinsulation.com/sites/corporate.knaufinsulation.net/files /Mineral%20wool%20with%20ECOSE%20Techn.pdf.

8. Dan Pink, TED talk based on his 2011 book *Drive*, http://www.ted.com /talks/dan_pink_on_motivation.html.

9. Ibid.

10. See, for example, Daniel H. Pink's excellent book *A Whole New Mind: Why Right-Brainers Will Rule the Future* (New York: Riverhead Books, 2006), on the power of left- and right-brain capabilities in business.

11. The fascinating world of cultural creatives is explored in Paul H. Ray and Sherry Ruth Anderson's book *The Cultural Creatives: How 50 Million People Are Changing the World* (New York: Three Rivers Press, 2000).

12. The difference between the decision mind-set and the design mind-set was best described in the book *Managing as Designing*, by Richard Boland Jr. and Fred Collopy (Stanford, CA: Stanford University Press, 2004).

13. Tim Brown, *Change by Design: How Design Thinking Transforms Organizations and Inspires Innovation* (New York: HarperCollins, 2009).

Chapter 8. The Death of Green, or, Is Your Marriage Sustainable?

1. GMA and Deloitte, *Finding the Green in Today's Shoppers: Sustainability Trends and New Shopper Insights*, 2009, https://www.deloitte.com/assets /Dcom-Lebanon/Local%20Assets/Documents/Consumer%20Business /DeloitteGreenShopperStudy_2009.pdf.

2. See BBMG, *2009 BBMG Conscious Consumer Report: Redefining Value in a New Economy*, casefoundation.org/blog/how-conscious-consumers-are -redefining-value-new-economy-8701.

3. World Economic Forum, *Redesigning Business Value: A Roadmap for Sustainable Consumption*, January 2010, http://www.weforum.org/pdf /sustainableconsumption/DrivingSustainableConsumptionreport.pdf.

4. Susan Spencer, "GreenUp Faces Uphill Battle," *Worcester Telegram & Gazette*, February 6, 2012, http://www.telegram.com/article/20120205 /NEWS/102059792/-1/NEWS07.

5. Gregory Unruh, "No, Consumers Will Not Pay More for Green," *Forbes*, July 28, 2011, http://www.forbes.com/sites/csr/2011/07/28/no-consumers -will-not-pay-more-for-green/.

6. Jonathan P. Doh et al., "Does the Market Respond to an Endorsement of Social Responsibility? The Role of Institutions, Information, and Legitimacy," *Journal of Management* 36, no. 6 (November 2010): 1461–85, http://jom .sagepub.com/content/36/6/1461.abstract.

7. See the entire 2011 Trendwatching.com trend report at http://www .trendwatching.com/trends/11trends2011/#eco.

8. Jack Neff, "As More Marketers Go Green, Fewer Consumers Willing to Pay For It," *Advertising Age*, September 24, 2012, http://adage.com/article/news /marketers-green-fewer-consumers-pay/237377/.

9. This and many other great discoveries are courtesy of *Fast Company*—see, for example, the July/August 2013 issue, http://www.fastcompany.com /magazine/177/july-august-2013.

10. You can read the whole story of the Tennant Company in a wonderful 2012 teaching case, *Tennant Company: Can "Chemical-Free" Be a Pathway to Competitive Advantage?* by Garima Sharma, Chris Laszlo, Eric Ahearn, and Indrajeet Ghatge (London, Ontario, Canada: Ivey Publishing, 2012), http:// hbr.org/product/tennant-company-can-chemical-free-be-a-pathway-to -/an/W12808-PDF-ENG.

11. J. Lester Federer, "20_SeeChange Health," Most Innovative Companies 2013, *Fast Company*, February 11, 2013, http://www.fastcompany.com /most-innovative-companies/2013/seechange-health.

12. See "10. Eco-Superior," Trendwatching.com, http://www.trendwatching.com /trends/11trends2011/#eco.

Chapter 9. As a Means of Conclusion: What Should Business Do?

1. Carolyn Aiken and Scott Keller, "The Irrational Side of Change Management," *McKinsey Quarterly*, April 2009, http://www.mckinsey.com/insights /organization/the_irrational_side_of_change_management.

2. Roger L. Martin, "The Execution Trap," *Harvard Business Review*, July 2010, 64–71.

3. Ibid.

4. The entire article is worth reading; see Karl Moore, "Porter or Mintzberg: Whose View of Strategy Is the Most Relevant Today?" *Forbes*, March 28, 2011, at http://www.forbes.com/sites/karlmoore/2011/03/28/porter-or -mintzberg-whose-view-of-strategy-is-the-most-relevant-today/.

5. Ibid.

6. These quotes and data for Walmart stories came from a DVD I purchased from Walmart in 2006 or early 2007. Produced by Walmart and titled "Sustainability 101," it has been a great addition to my executive education classes ever since. On January 13, 2014, I was able to access it online in full at http://greenenergytv.com/watch.php?v=367.

7. For more on Shell's scenario planning, see "What Are Scenarios?" Shell Global, http://www.shell.com/global/future-energy/scenarios/what-are -scenarios.html.

Index

About the Author

Dr. Nadya Zhexembayeva is a business owner, author, and educator working at the intersection of innovation, leadership, and sustainable growth.

As a business owner, Nadya oversees a group of companies active in real estate, investment, and consulting industries. Her recent client engagements include The Coca-Cola Company, ENRC PLC, Erste Bank, Henkel, Knauf Insulation, and Vienna Insurance Group.

Nadya also serves as the Coca-Cola Chaired Professor of Sustainable Development at IEDC- Bled School of Management, an executive education center based in Slovene Alps, where she teaches courses in leadership, strategy, change management, design thinking, and sustainability. In addition to IEDC, Dr. Zhexembayeva has taught in a number of other business schools, including CEDEP-INSEAD (France) and IPADE (Mexico).

Dr. Zhexembayeva chairs Resourcefulness Advisory Board at OMV, an oil and gas company, and sits on the Advisory Board of Fowler Center for Sustainable Value at Weatherhead School of Management, Case Western Reserve University. She also serves as Vice-President of Challenge:Future, a global student think-DO-tank and innovation competition.

"Overfished Ocean Strategy: Powering Up Innovation for Resource-Deprived World" is Nadya's second book. Together with Chris Laszlo, in 2011, Dr. Zhexembayeva co-authored her first book, "Embedded Sustainability: The Next Big Competitive Advantage," published by Stanford University Press in the US and Greenleaf Publishing in the UK.

A daughter of Kazakhstan, these days Nadya and her family split their life between US and Europe.

Berrett–Koehler
Publishers

Berrett-Koehler is an independent publisher dedicated to an ambitious mission: *Creating a World That Works for All*.

We believe that to truly create a better world, action is needed at all levels—individual, organizational, and societal. At the individual level, our publications help people align their lives with their values and with their aspirations for a better world. At the organizational level, our publications promote progressive leadership and management practices, socially responsible approaches to business, and humane and effective organizations. At the societal level, our publications advance social and economic justice, shared prosperity, sustainability, and new solutions to national and global issues.

A major theme of our publications is "Opening Up New Space." Berrett-Koehler titles challenge conventional thinking, introduce new ideas, and foster positive change. Their common quest is changing the underlying beliefs, mindsets, institutions, and structures that keep generating the same cycles of problems, no matter who our leaders are or what improvement programs we adopt.

We strive to practice what we preach—to operate our publishing company in line with the ideas in our books. At the core of our approach is stewardship, which we define as a deep sense of responsibility to administer the company for the benefit of all of our "stakeholder" groups: authors, customers, employees, investors, service providers, and the communities and environment around us.

We are grateful to the thousands of readers, authors, and other friends of the company who consider themselves to be part of the "BK Community." We hope that you, too, will join us in our mission.

A BK Business Book

This book is part of our BK Business series. BK Business titles pioneer new and progressive leadership and management practices in all types of public, private, and nonprofit organizations. They promote socially responsible approaches to business, innovative organizational change methods, and more humane and effective organizations.

Berrett–Koehler
Publishers

A community dedicated to creating
a world that works for all

Dear Reader,

Thank you for picking up this book and joining our worldwide community of Berrett-Koehler readers. We share ideas that bring positive change into people's lives, organizations, and society.

To welcome you, we'd like to offer you a free e-book. You can pick from among twelve of our bestselling books by entering the promotional code **BKP92E** here: http://www.bkconnection.com/welcome.

When you claim your free e-book, we'll also send you a copy of our e-newsletter, the *BK Communiqué*. Although you're free to unsubscribe, there are many benefits to sticking around. In every issue of our newsletter you'll find

- A free e-book
- Tips from famous authors
- Discounts on spotlight titles
- Hilarious insider publishing news
- A chance to win a prize for answering a riddle

Best of all, our readers tell us, "Your newsletter is the only one I actually read." So claim your gift today, and please stay in touch!

Sincerely,

Charlotte Ashlock
Steward of the BK Website

Questions? Comments? Contact me at bkcommunity@bkpub.com.

Certified

Corporation
bcorporation.net